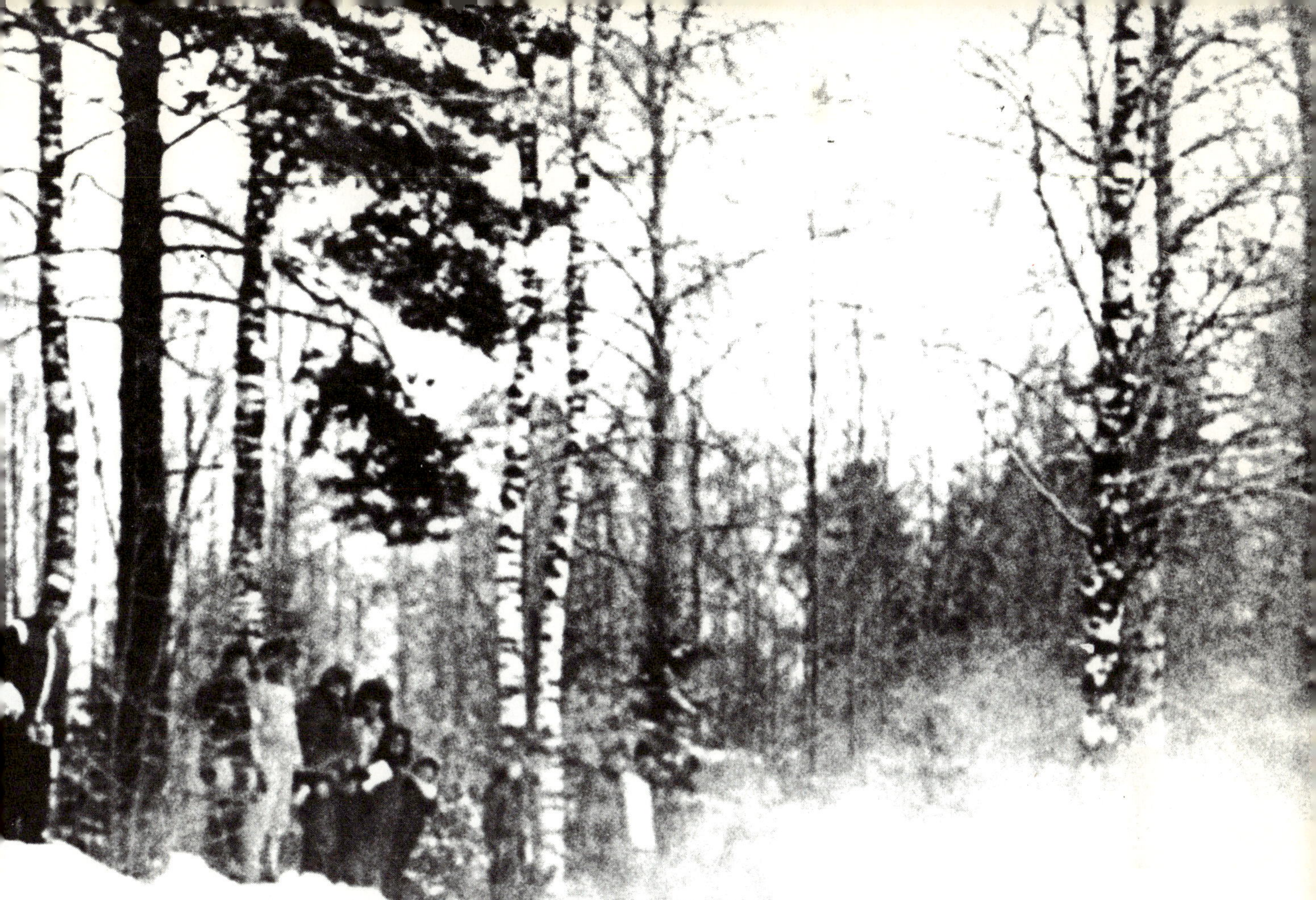

DRIVE IT!

The Complete Book of

RALLYING

Stuart Turner
& Tony Mason

ISBN 0 85429 240 3

First published October 1978

A FOULIS Motoring Book

Published by
Haynes Publishing Group
Sparkford, Yeovil, Somerset BA22 7JJ, England

Distributed in North America by:
Haynes Publications Inc
861 Lawrence Drive, Newbury Park, California 91320 USA

Editor: Rod Grainger
Layout design: John Martin and Charlie Wharton
Dust jacket design: Phill Jennings
Printed and bound by: Haynes Publishing Group

Contents

Foreword

I am delighted that rallying has now been included in the *Drive it!* series. And not before time, I say, because it is one of the finest and most challenging sports there is.

I've been lucky enough to make a career of rallying for more years than I care to remember; for many of those years I've worked with Stuart Turner and Tony Mason and both have become close friends. They have one thing in common — they've spent most of their time telling me what to do (often in no uncertain terms!) — Stuart as team chief and Tony as a co-driver (including what I will always count as one of my favourite wins — the 1972 R.A.C. Rally).

I'm pleased to see that they work together just as well as authors. They have packed a lot of information into this book; I hope it will encourage more people to take up rallying and, hopefully, to get as much enjoyment out of the sport as I have.

Roger Clark

Introduction

If you have picked up this book in a shop because you are mildly curious about rallying but have never actually competed – congratulations! Congratulations because you have stumbled on one of the most exciting and exhilarating sports there is.

Perhaps we'd better start by making it clear exactly what a motor rally is. It is *not* a mass gathering in Trafalgar Square addressed by Vanessa Redgrave (aren't they all?) nor is a rally a race.

A rally means visiting a number of places within given time limits. Cars usually start at minute intervals and every car in a rally has the same time allowance for each section of the route. Obviously, if every driver in a particular rally did every section within the time limits set then they would all be equal winners, which would be a farce. To guard against this happening, rallies include special stages which are over roads closed to other traffic (such as private farm tracks or Forestry Commission land) and over which cars are timed against the clock.

Some rallies may have just one or two tests to sort out competitors; others like the R.A.C. or Monte Carlo rallies are settled entirely on stage results. This means that unless freak weather causes havoc on a rally, the results will normally depend on which is the fastest – or most reliable – car with the best driver.

Almost all European motor manufacturers are involved in rallying in some way or another and they compete for two reasons – development and publicity. A rally driver sweating after the glory (and cash!) of a major rally win will push a car far harder than most development engineers and rallying also makes an ideal testing ground for supporting manufacturers – tyres, lights and brakes are just a few examples.

Although top flight rallying is highly professional, it is still accessible to a private competitor who tackles his rallying in a sensible way. This is one of the attractions of the sport – its heroes are within reach of Mr Averageman. Anyone taking up rallying for the first time could reasonably expect to be competing on international events without disgracing himself within eighteen months.

We use 'himself' throughout the book for brevity incidentally, but it could just as well be 'herself'. Throughout the history of rallying there have been one or two women quite capable of finishing high up results tables. In fact, with today's constant search for sponsorship to offset rising costs, women drivers possibly have a better chance than men of reaching the upper echelons because of their attraction for sponsors.

However, this book isn't really about the upper echelons of rallying, attractive though they may be. Instead it is intended as a basic guide for someone taking up the sport from scratch.

Most amateur golfers have enough of the Walter Mitty in them to dream of winning the Open. Similarly when things are going well and a car is flowing over a special stage, lots of rally drivers must think that, given the breaks, they could be up there scrapping with the Scandinavians. And so they could: if they show enough application and determination. Many of the drivers mentioned in this book are within a few years of retirement, so the future looks bright for newcomers. And even if you don't want to become a top line professional rally driver but only do the sport for fun, then you will still get more enjoyment out of your hobby if you go about it in the right way – by getting the right equipment, by studying your driving technique, by preparing your car properly and by tackling the right rallies, in the right order.

In other words, by doing all the things which this book will hopefully teach you.

1 The history

Rally drivers rarely stop to consider the history of their sport preferring, rightly, to concentrate on preparations for their next event. Nevertheless, rallying has a long and reasonably noble history.

Purists may disagree but really the very first motoring events – such as the Paris to Rouen in 1894 and the Paris-Bordeaux-Paris in 1895 – were rallies, even though they were called races or reliability trials. They were rallies because in those early days of motoring the *challenge* of actually getting to a place was one of the main incentives, the time taken or the overall position being secondary.

Cars in those events back at the turn of the century carried passengers, just like modern rally cars; they were set off at intervals, just like modern rally cars, and there was a certain amount of navigation or route finding involved, again just as on many modern rallies. The main difference of course was that in those days there was more excitement in motoring; more of a sense of pioneering. Not so today, when any moment parking seems likely to be made a capital offence!

Although France staged the first motor sport events, we must turn to Germany for the next milestone in any history of rallying because in 1904 Germany saw the Herkomer Trophy, which was a long distance regularity contest for touring cars. Competitors had to maintain strict average speeds between controls, which had to be visited in the right order. Sadly, the regulations were too complex and the rally finished in a flurry of arguments. One thing has thus remained constant throughout the history of rallying – if organisers try to be too clever, competitors will either try to find a way round the regulations or bitch about the results at the finish! All organisers should have a sign on their desks saying "Our job is to provide enjoyment for drivers".

Anyway, getting back to Germany, the Herkomer Trophy faded after a few years but the "Prinz Heinrich Fahrt" took its place. To their everlasting credit, the Imperial Automobile Club persuaded Prince Heinrich of Prussia to put his name to their event – and bear in mind that this was at a time when Germany had just introduced a car tax and speed limits.

The Automobile Club had 130 starters for their first event in 1908, including a couple of fellows not without connections with the motor industry – Bugatti and Opel. After seven days and fourteen-thousand miles the winner was Fritz Erle in a Benz.

The rally spurred the Austrians into organising something similar and their Internationale Alpenfahrt started in 1910. The event grew in stature and by 1914 was attracting entries from all over Europe, including Rolls-Royce.

While the Germans and Austrians were busy building up their events, further south businessmen in Monte Carlo had watched the increasing popularity of the motor car and considered that an event in January might help fill their hotels at a slack period. So a major milestone in rallying took place with the first Monte Carlo Rally in 1911. The organiser's sensible aim was to get as many people to Monte Carlo as possible and it was much less challenging than the event we know today. Nevertheless some of the elements of today's rally were there, with cars starting from several starting points throughout Europe.

After a disastrous Monte in 1924, when they switched to March, the rally really took hold from 1925 and during the Thirties regularly had over 150 starters. Perhaps January has always been a slow news month for sport – and there are worse places to be in the winter than Monte Carlo – as a result the event has always had wide media attention and even today is perhaps the best known motoring event in Europe.

Perhaps the most important year for British rally enthusiasts was 1929 because that was when the R.A.C. Rally started, although as it was a fairly gentle tour with just a few driving tests, it bore little resemblance to today's glorious thrash through the forests.

Two years later, in 1931, the Royal Motor Union of Liège ran their first Marathon de la Route. The organisers were firm believers in 'no nonsense' rallies with the challenge coming from long and difficult routes, not from nit-picking regulations. In 1951 the event became the Liège-Rome-Liège, then when roads became too crowded over that route, they switched in 1956 to Liège-Sofia-Liège. If you want to see grown men cry, mention "The Liège" to any of the current rally stars who were lucky enough to do it. The sheer challenge of around ninety-hours of virtually non-stop motoring over dusty roads in Yugoslavia and Bulgaria was quite something.

The other 'classic' which deserves an honourable mention in any history is the Alpine, or to give it its full title "The Coupe des Alpes". This started in 1949 and through to its demise in the early 1970s provided a tough menu of special sections over mountain passes — so much so that a 'Coupe' for a penalty free run rightly became the most cherished prize in the sport.

The late 1950s saw a gradual but positive shift among competitors from amateur to professional (in attitude if not earning power) or if you like, from gentlemen to players. Happily it happened without any interference from promotors. The sport has always been free of squabbles over amateurs and professionals, possibly because it has always been so expensive that even the wealthy competitors have been glad to accept help! We are not suggesting that rally drivers before the Fifties were not serious, obviously they were, but the new breed were virtually full-time professionals earning their living at the sport and therefore able to spend a lot of time practising.

The second big change seen in the late Fifties was the start of the Scandinavian invasion. Eric Carlsson was the pioneering angel and his exploits with the Saab became legendary — "The biggest driver in the smallest car" was a journalist's dream.

Rauno Aaltonen was one of the next Scandinavians to make an impact (arriving from a co-driver's seat in the Mercedes team) and then of course they came in hordes.

No-one has really explained why; perhaps the roads in Sweden and Finland give them plenty of opportunity to practise; perhaps the long dark nights do something to the soul which makes good rally drivers. Whatever it is (and if you could bottle it you could make a fortune) you have to accept that, despite the giant efforts of Russell Brookes, Tony Pond and Roger Clark, the Scandinavians are still the ones to beat.

If we jump forward ten years to the late Sixties we see the last change in our history — the growth of sponsorship. Rallying became perhaps more democratic and as youngsters with more ability than cash fought to reach the top, they naturally turned to sponsors to lubricate their efforts. People like Castrol and Shell and others had long supported people in racing and rallying but they suddenly realised that they would

Early motor races and reliability trials could really be considered as rallies.

An almost standard Standard on a 1959 Monte Carlo Rally. Roof mounted spotlights are now banned. Note the outside horns!

One of the classic rally cars – the Austin Healey 3000 seen here on Mont Ventoux on the 1962 Alpine Rally.

Leader of the Scandinavian invasion Eric Carlsson comes up to a standing ovation with his Saab after his first R.A.C. Rally win.

get better value if more people were aware of their involvement – hence the sponsors decal (orsticker). More recently, cars have appeared in properly planned total colour schemes.

With the advent of sponsors – particularly those from non-motoring areas who brought in fresh ideas – came professional public relations and with it better media coverage. Rallying still doesn't receive proper media attention, though what there is gets increasingly international with Swedish TV covering the Safari, German TV covering the R.A.C. Rally and so on. All good stuff for manufacturers and sponsors.

Other historical milestones? The growth of stage events at the expense of road rallies in Britain – inevitable with crowded roads and faster cars, but still sad. Apart from anything else road rallies provide a great training ground and they have even attracted members of the Royal Family as competitors which does the sport no harm at all.

Safety has improved, which has to be a very good thing. Then 1978 saw the re-birth of one-make championships designed to keep costs down – also a good thing because it means that team managers looking for talent can study the results knowing that Fred is quick because he is a better driver, not because he has spent more on his car than Albert.

In summary, therefore, most of the changes throughout the history of rallying have been gradual and sensible. Go forth young man knowing your sport has a good pedigree!

2 Types of rallies

Although no two rallies are alike it is possible to place them in certain categories; at one end of the scale the small club social rally and at the other the glamorous, rugged full-blown International. Each type has its own specialists, its own fans and its own champions. The various types require different skills from competitors and perhaps the only constant factor is that a *reliable* car of some sort is needed for success, speed and performance being less critical on many events.

You will need a car, driver and a co-driver/navigator/passenger for any rally but it is impossible to generalise on role the of the person occupying the passenger seat; certainly it is difficult to adjudicate on the ratio of importance between driver and navigator. On a rally where there are numerous navigational problems, the responsibility for success falls fairly and squarely on the navigator: as long as the driver can operate the controls of the car there is no reason why he should not chauffeur his able colleague to victory.

It is also possible for an unbalanced crew to win another type of rally altogether – a good special stage driver can frequently win a very simple stage rally even if accompanied by a very simple co-driver. There has even been facetious talk of co-drivers being replaced by sacks of potatoes on easier stage rallies!.

However these are the extremes and the basic recipe for success in rallying is a good combination of crew talents plus a reliable vehicle, one prepared with care and attention to detail.

Let's now look at the different types of event, starting in the lower echelons and working up to the world-famous rallies. We hope devotees of the car treasure-hunt wil forgive us if we start with their particular event which is often regarded as the lowest end of the scale.

Whenever social groups gather, a car treasure hunt is likely to find itself on their social calendar. Most countries have regulations controlling the running of events on public highways and Britain is no exception. It is against the law to run any unauthorised motoring event of more than twelve cars on the public highway wherein the driver may receive any form of time penalty. Therefore, organisers of treasure hunts can break the law unless they take care. Nevertheless it is still possible to organise successful treasure hunts which stay well within the law, yet provide innocent entertainment for the participants.

Treasure hunts tend to take place in daylight hours and the basic requirement is to solve clues or gather pieces of information as the car travels round a gentle route. The route itself may be given by clues and questions; some organisers lay on a mobile *Times* crossword, others prefer a more light-hearted approach.

Treasure hunts have sometimes caused problems with reports of disturbances in sleepy villages, ranging from the desecration of churchyards to the interruption of retired Colonels' Sunday afternoon naps, but *if* (and *only* if) treasure hunts are organised with care they can be good fun and can even be regarded as good navigator training. They certainly provide mental exercise.

Despite the social nature of the treasure hunt, prospective organisers would do well to advise the police of the passage of the event and might find the event more acceptable if the crews are not required to leave the cars too often. Great care should, of course, be taken with the use of narrow lanes in the route.

The only rallies which do not require full authorisation from the Royal Automobile Club (who act on behalf of the Department of the Environment) are those in which twelve cars or less compete. Even so, these events are subject to some restrictions and organisers must advise the police and the R.A.C. of any event that is planned.

The organisation of a twelve car rally is obviously much easier than a bigger one, and although entry lists can never be numerically strong, the events are popular with motor clubs who frequently run them as

A major force in rallying – Pentti Airikkala and the Chevette seen here on the way to a win in a Mintex Rally.

Eric Davies and Allan Jones with their Vauxhall on the 1978 Cambrian News Rally.

training events for less experienced members. As they are usually run to the rigid rules of the bigger events, they make a good starting point for the raw beginner. They are often short in distance and will probably take place during an evening. Like most road events, it is advisable to run them during darkness as the narrow lanes of Britain are less than ideal for safe competition motoring in daylight hours. Sadly in some areas, twelve car rallies have overstayed their welcome and there has been talk of banning them.

Moving on from twelve car events, the 'closed-to-club' rally is next on the agenda. This event will be organised to conform to all the rules and regulations applying to any major road rally; the route will have to be authorised in detail but participation in the event will be restricted to members of the promoting club only. The mileage will probably not be very great but neither will the expense of competing (nor the awards for that matter!). It is not necessary to have an R.A.C. competition licence in order to compete in a 'closed-to-club' rally; all you need is a Club membership card.

There are two basic types of rally in Britain. One is the road rally where the car and crew are required to pass given points at specified times and spend the entire period of the rally on public roads. Naturally a restriction on the maximum required average speed is imposed to avoid racing on the public highway or exceeding statutory limits.

The other type of event is the special stage rally where cars enjoy relatively easy public road sections but are required to cover stages on private land at high speeds. It is very much a 'Jekyll and Hyde' operation as drivers have to cope with gentle road sections then fierce and fast stages. The stages can be found on private farm tracks, disused airfields and railway lines or in the magnificent forest tracks of Britain. Enterprising organisers have been known to use private roads in stately homes, factories, the roads around sewerage plants, and believe it or not, the subterranean tracks of a coal-mine. The latter was featured on a Swedish rally many moons ago, but then there are no bounds to the imagination of rally organisers in Sweden and Finland. Scandinavian rally stages frequently traverse frozen lakes and rivers, sometimes with the stage carved out of the snow on a lake's frozen surface by a snow plough a few hours before the cars are due.

British stages can be muddy, rocky and rough, but are very popular with competitors even in spite of the higher costs of competing on a stage rally rather than a road event.

Probably the most popular grade of rally is the 'Restricted' club rally. Here a club will extend an invitation to other neighbouring or prominent motor clubs whose members will be entitled to compete in the event upon production of a current club membership card plus the competition licence of the appropriate grade.

The successor to the big Healeys – the TR7 driven here on a Scottish Rally by Tony Pond.

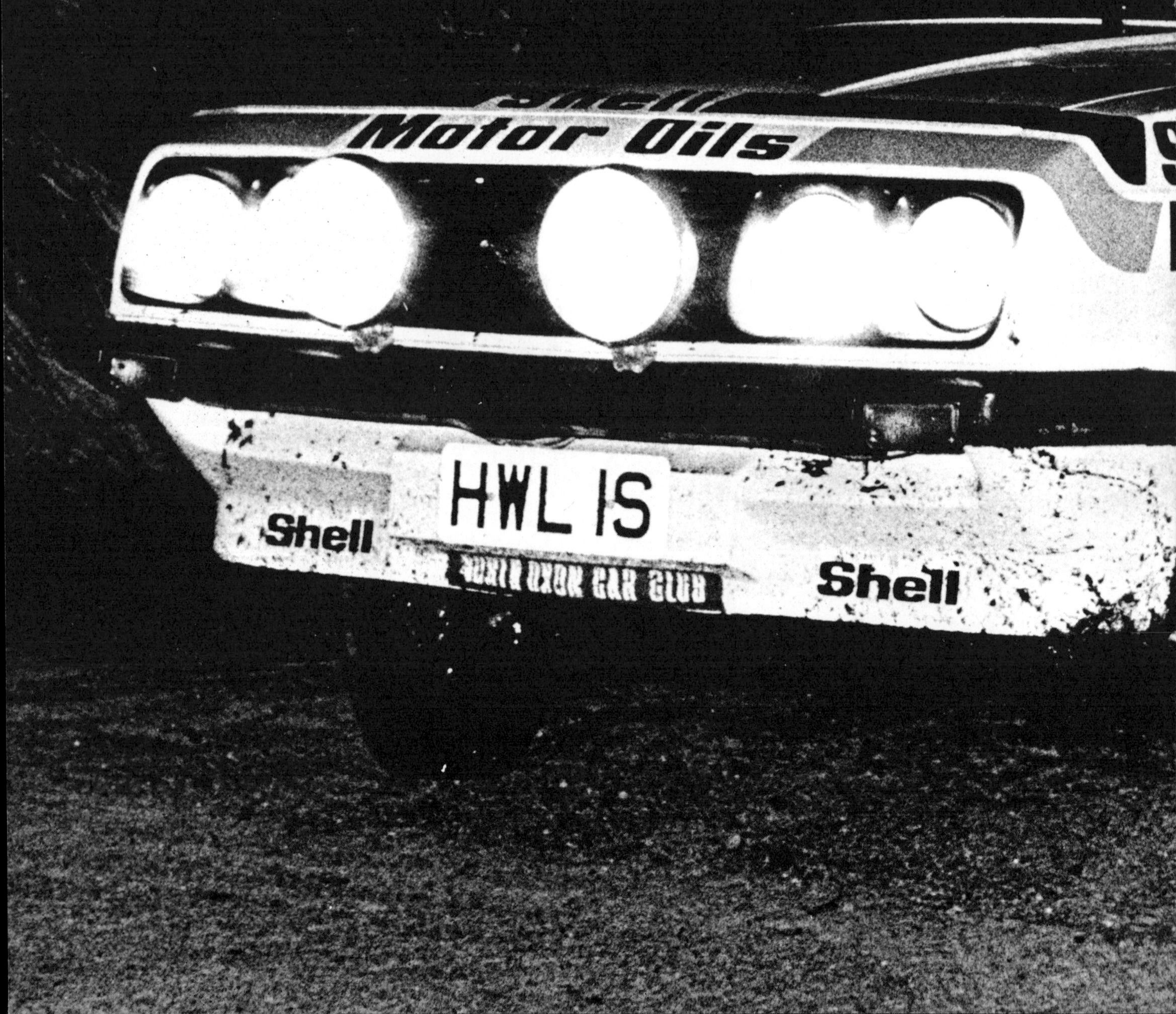
Motor Oils
Shell
Shell

One of Britain's best road rally crews, Bill Gwynne and Terry Thorp negotiate a hairpin bend in Wales. Note the use of an intercom.

Stage and road rallies are both popular at Restricted grade and usually last one full day (in the case of stage events) or one full night (in case of both) rather than the half day or half night of lesser events.

As Restricted rallies are run to R.A.C. regulations it is necessary for competing cars to conform to all the requirements laid down by the R.A.C., so they will have to pass the inspection of a Scrutineer before the event starts. Stage and road events have different requirements but all relate to safety, be it the safety of competitors or that of spectators.

Noise level is an important factor in the case of all road rallies and cars are scrutineered before the start of any event. Should an exhaust system be damaged or develop a fault during an event, the crew will probably find themselves penalised or excluded by noise marshals who lurk in the lanes.

Road rallies up to Restricted level may have the routes defined by map references or more intricate methods. Either way, the navigator will play an important role. On a really difficult navigational event the person in the passenger seat plays by far *the* more important part. Most of the route will confine itself to lanes and byways, some non-surfaced and occasionally non-charted. Some sections, on the more deserted parts of the route, may be timed to the second but there are restrictions on the number of 'selective' sections allowed. 'Selectives', by the way, should only be run after midnight. Maps will be of great importance and almost certainly the excellent Ordnance Survey maps will be used.

Numerous road rally Championships exist, won by performance on selected events which qualify: in some championships competitors have to register to qualify, in others they score automatically if they finish in a scoring position. There are area championships, inter-club championships and even national championships devoted to road rallies. By far the best known is the Motoring News Rally Championship which has run without a break since 1960 while the B.T.R.D.A. Silver Star Championship has run from even earlier than that – see what we meant earlier by the sport having a noble history?

Incidentally one area of training for navigators which, for some reason, is rarely mentioned in motoring

A good sponsor to have for an expensive sport!

circles is the growing sport of orienteering. Orienteers are required to visit various points on a map — on foot by the way — covering different types of terrain, reaching the finish within a specified time. Motor rallying and orienteering both have a fanatical following in Scandinavia and the whole question of map reading, course plotting and "reading the countryside" is common to both. The only difference is that the orienteering map reader does not need a car or driver (many navigators might interpret this as a distinct advantage!) No one would seriously describe orienteering as a type of car rally but as a navigational training exercise it is worth more than a passing thought. Many drivers are far from physically fit — maybe they, too, could benefit from a spot of orienteering!

Although road rallies in Britain will not be found at any level higher than Restricted grade, it is worth mentioning that some European events attract British road rally addicts. There are numerous small tarmac events, particularly in Belgium, of at least one night's duration which present good value as they are inexpensive by International standards. Further incentives are often given by the organisers who arrange free entries, cheap hotel accommodation and even low cost ferry fares.

Stage rallies operate at all grades in Britain, the Restricted grade being by far the most common. Many of these rallies have access to the wide variety of loose surface tracks in Britain's forests. Although the Forestry Commission has stringent rules about the amount of use each road may have, as well as on the charges to be levied on organisers and routes to be taken, however without the use of these tracks the British rally scene would be a lot poorer and have far less capable drivers in its ranks.

The level of crew responsibility changes in the case of stage rallies, the driver assuming a far more important role. The car must be tough and well prepared, and will probably need greater performance than its road rally counterpart. Tyre patterns become more important and conversation turns to differentials, cams, special driveshafts, five-speed gearboxes and the like.

Total stage mileage can range from twenty-five to one-hundred miles or more and the road mileage can

Stalwarts of British rallying — John Bloxham and Richard Harper on the Cilwendeg Rally.

A closed road stage on an Irish rally always brings out the crowds. This is John Taylor on a Galway Rally.

Sections of the famous Manx TT course are included in the Manx Trophy Rally.

One of the world's longest rallies – the 1970 London to Mexico won by Hannu Mikkola and Gunnar Palm.

be literally anything; it will probably consist of main road or even motorway driving at times, all totally non-competitive.

On a stage rally the pressure is really on the driver to drive as quickly as possible from the start of each stage to the finish. The length of the stages varies from a mere mile or two to twenty miles or more, although anything above twenty is rare. Organisers should always place prominent arrows at junctions and bends, and mark hazard spots on the track and in the road book; start and finish points are clearly marked by large boards, too. The navigator, who is now starting to assume the role of co-driver (we shall discuss the delicate terminology later) has to keep an eye on the whole proceedings though he won't have to find the route from the map (although some co-drivers on British events found that following marked maps of forests helped their driver considerably – which led to their use being banned on many events!). However, the co-driver will keep an eye on the stage and help confirm arrows to his driver. He will tell him how far it is to the finish in the event of a puncture so that the driver can decide whether to stop or limp on, and he will check the time carefully on arrival at the finish of a stage. There are stage target times, times of arrival and departure at stages, petrol halts, road controls, etc., to think about so the co-driver is kept fully occupied.

National special stage rallies have a minimum stage total of sixty miles and are open to any national competition licence holder. They tend to concentrate on forestry roads and consist entirely of special stages. These full day or full night events usually attract a big entry of well-prepared cars, all of which conform to the regulations stipulated for a national event. The rallies take place in all parts of the United Kingdom and usually qualify for a major championship.

There are now a number of British International forest rallies – other than the famed Lombard R.A.C. – and it is the aim of many Clubmen to compete in one of these events during their rally careers. Using the best of the forest tracks available to them, these events enjoy a high standard of organisation, and although they seldom attract more than a handful of overseas drivers, they do give Britons the taste of International rally conditions. The Welsh and Scottish are by far the best known of these lesser internationals. British works and dealer teams and the occasional overseas works team enter these events, giving them reasonable International flavour.

The pinnacle in Britain is of course the Lombard R.A.C. Since its move to the forests in 1961 the R.A.C. has grown from strength-to-strength and now enjoys the healthiest entry list of any rally in the world. All the top drivers rate it as one of their favourite events and the unpractised forests certainly put all the drivers on an even footing. It has become firmly established as a major spectator and sporting event in Britain and over two million people turn out to watch the five day rally each year; millions more follow it on TV and radio.

Before leaving the British scene, mention must be made of the very popular and extremely demanding tarmac rallies. Thanks to the favourable views of their governments to closing public roads, Ireland and the Isle of Man provide opportunities for British drivers to gain the sort of experience once only available to Continentals. Ireland boasts the Easter weekend Circuit of Ireland, as well as the Donegal and Galway rallies and the Isle of Man produces the Manx International each Autumn. The events are pure stage rallies and most cars run on racing tyres and even lowered suspension. Events last three or four days; and thanks to the high speeds and unforgiving bumps, often have fewer finishers than any forest rally of comparable length.

Mainland Europe still plays host to the World Rally Circus for half the rally year; there are numerous major events held in the classic mountains of Europe, and very demanding they are too. Some British Club drivers make sorties to compete in these European events, particularly the small International rallies in Spain, Portugal or Southern France, as these can be combined with a holiday.

The world of rallying has spread its wings and there are major events in every corner of the world. Large countries with sparse populations permit long, fast open road sections, and on African rallies cars can go for hours without ever touching an asphalt road.

Developing countries are keen to add rallying to their list of attractions and the African and Middle east countries are now employing the talents of British rally organisers to get them on their feet.

National speed limits and other restrictions result in rallies of a more navigational nature in America although some stage rallies do take place; and Californian laws allow road and stage rallies to be run with little difficulty. There are numerous rallies in the Eastern Bloc countries and the U.S.S.R. sends its State Rally Team on periodic sorties outside the Soviet Union. The son of the Prime Minister of Poland is among its rally stars.

So regardless of politics, creed or colour, there are rallies in every corner of the world. There are rallies on minute islands in the Southern Hemisphere, there are rallies hundreds of miles north of the Arctic Circle. And, if that is not enough, there are the trans-world marathons.

One thing *all* rallies have in common – you need a car. And it is now time for a mild dose of rally jargon as we look at such things as "groups" and "homologation".

Andrew Cowan winning the 1977 London to Sydney Rally in a Mercedes-Benz – nine years after he won the first in a Hillman Hunter.

3 Group therapy

Before a car can compete on a major rally it must be homologated (for sporting purposes) by its manufacturer. Homologation is not as painful as it sounds. It simply means listing the technical details of a car (so they can be checked by a scrutineer) on a Form of Recognition – in effect a 'birth certificate' for the car.

The Form of Recognition defines the construction of the car and the modifications allowed and must carry the signature of a senior Director of the company to ensure it complies with the Rules of the FIA Sporting Code. So in theory there should be no cheating!

For rallying cars can be homologated into one of five groups depending on the type of car and/or what modifications have subsequently taken place and it's worth wading through until you understand the Groups because they are part of rally jargon:

Group 1:   Large volume production cars made in at least 5000 identical units per year. Apart from safety items, very few subsequent modifications are allowed – mainly 'blue printing'. Under this for instance the engine can be fine tuned to its best production specification by bringing things to their blue printed dimensions.
Examples: *Ford Escort RS 2000*
                      Leyland Dolomite Sprint

Group 2:   These cars are usually modified Group 1 cars, or they can be specialist cars built at the rate of 1000 identical units per annum. The basic form of the car cannot be changed but freedom is left to suit the car to particular events (for example, wider wheels for racing) although the basic configuration of the suspension cannot be changed.

Group 3:   Large volume sports cars – 1000 units per year and the same limitations as Group 1 with respect to allowed modifications
Example: *MGB*   *TR7*
                   Porsche 911

Group 4:   Low volume specialised cars – 400 units produced in 24 consecutive months. The modifications allowed are the same as for Group 2, but because these cars start life as more exotic and expensive cars the final modified competition car is much quicker than a Group 2 car. This is the Group which provides most of the rally winners!
Examples: *Fiat Abarth 131*   *Ford Escort RS*
                      Lancia Stratos
                      Vauxhall Chevette 2300HS

FÉDÉRATION INTERNATIONALE DE L'AUTOMOBILE

FICHE D'HOMOLOGATION CONFORME A L'ANNEXE J DU CODE SPORTIF INTERNATIONAL
POUR LES VOITURES DES GROUPES 1 A 5

BOOK OF RECOGNITION IN ACCORDANCE WITH APPENDIX J TO THE INTERNATIONAL
SPORTING CODE FOR CARS OF GROUPS 1 TO 5

Constructeur/Manufacturer ___FORD___ Modèle / Model ___ESCORT RS___

Cylindrée / Cylinder capacity ___1975___ cc

Constructeur du châssis / Chassis Manufacturer ___FORD___

Constructeur du moteur / Engine Manufacturer ___FORD___

Homologation valable à partir du / Recognition valid as from ___1.4.77.___

Modèle homologué en groupe ___4___
Model recognized in group

Numéro d'homologation ___650___
Recognition number

Photo A : voiture vue de 3/4 AV
Photo A : 3/4 view of car from front

Photo B : voiture vue de 3/4 AR
Photo B : 3/4 view of car from rear

CARACTÉRISTIQUES GÉNÉRALES / GENERAL CHARACTERISTICS :

1) Mode de construction : construction séparée / monocoque.
   Type of car construction : separate / unitary construction.

2) Matériau du châssis ___STEEL___   Matériau de la carrosserie ___STEEL___
   Material of chassis   Material of coachwork

3) Empattement droit ___2407 MM___   Gauche ___2407 MM___
   Wheelbase right   Left

4) Largeur de la carrosserie mesurée aux axes AV ___1664 MM___
   Width of bodywork measured at front axle

5) Largeur de la carrosserie mesurée aux axes AR ___1700 MM___
   Width of bodywork measured at rear axle

6) Longueur hors-tout avec pare-chocs ___3978 MM___ Sans pare-chocs ___3960 MM___
   Overall length with bumpers   Without bumpers

7) Type de suspension : AV ___Macpherson___ AR ___Live Axle with 5 Locating Links___
   Type of suspension : Front   Rear

   (Photo D)   (Photo E)

   Signature et cachet de   Signature et cachet
   l'autorité sportive nationale,   de la FIA

   C. S. I.

One page from an F.I.A. homologation form – virtually a 'birth certificate' for a car and essential before it can be used in major competition.

Finally, at least as far as rallying is concerned, there is —

Group 5: Highly modified cars which only bear a faint resemblance to the original production car, retaining only the overall body shape and cylinder block. Group 5 cars are mainly used in racing and are rarely found in the more dignified world of rallying

For World and European status Rally Championship events, cars can only belong to Groups 1, 2, 3 or 4.

Although rallying is relatively free from 'scandals', these groups, and homologation into them, represent something of a simmering volcano.

Manufacturers want to win, so they tend to take regulations to the limits and they may be optimistic on production quantities and the specification of their cars.

Then national pride creeps in. Homologation forms have to be vetted by National Clubs and if one Club sees a manufacturer in another country getting away with things, they may tend to let their own domestic manufacturers push their luck. And so it can spiral into a cheat's charter. While everyone is in a glass house, no-one is going to chuck protests about. Happily the problems won't affect 95% of competitors but if the sport is to stay clean and strong they need sorting out. Perhaps manufacturers should have to vet and 'sign - off' each others homologation forms?

Another problem in all Groups is that of policing the rules. It is not easy to prove or disprove the existence of 5000 identical cars in Group 1. With the wide choice of options offered today by most manufacturers, the chances of there being 5000 genuinely identical cars in this group are remote.

Then, of course, legislation in many countries is making it increasingly difficult to run anything but standard cars on the public highway and for this reason all major motor manufacturers are increasing their involvement in Group 1 — which will ultimately benefit private competitors. It is becoming too expensive for even large companies to build exotic Group 4 cars at the rate of 400 units in two years and still get them through the EEC regulations for use on the public highway.

The current trend (belatedly being resisted by the controlling bodies) is to bolster up the homologation paper for any one model with 'product variants' — rough road, emission, high altitude, performance options, etc, leaving the competitor free to choose the best selection of parts for his event. It is obvious that the existing rules are not working very well — it was never intended that variants could be mixed from one form, but it is asking the impossible that an unpaid scrutineer should be able to tell what part should be allowed with each variant package.

Our guess is that within a few years all cars will have to start off from Group 1 (i.e., 5000 per year) with other groups simply being further stages of modification of the base car. Sadly this may eliminate many of the exciting cars winning today but rallying cannot operate in a vacuum, disregarding the world about it.

So having digested that little lot, let's consider how to set about rallying.

4 How and where to start

If you want to take up rallying the first thing you must do is join a motor club which is 'recognised' by the R.A.C. To obtain recognition a club has to be reasonably well established and must operate in accordance with rules drawn up by the R.A.C. There are over eight-hundred recognised clubs in Britain and apart from providing a starting point for budding drivers and navigators they also offer a good social side.

The R.A.C. British Motor Sports Council, 31 Belgrave Square, London SW1X 8QH will be able to supply a list of clubs in your area or, better still, you should buy copies of their Year Books which include addresses of *all* motor clubs as well as a lot of other useful information.

Most clubs have a leaning towards one particular branch of the sport so if there are several in your area write to the secretaries to find out their main interests – as a budding rally driver it would make no sense to join a club specialising in hillclimbing.

Later in your rally career you will almost certainly join more than one club, including one of the major rally clubs so that you get invitations to the best rallies.

There are a handful of *national* clubs like the British Trial and Rally Drivers Association and the British Automobile Racing Club but most clubs are based in one particular locality and are linked with other clubs in their area to form Regional Associations of the R.A.C.

It is pretty certain that you will find a motor club based in your nearest town.

Each year the average motor club organises, or co-organises with neighbouring clubs, a handful of road and stage rallies of a "Closed-to-club" status and possibly one major Restricted rally as well; in addition it probably organises some twelve-car rallies. It will almost certainly hold regular club meetings, film shows and social functions.

Although you may have enjoyed spectating on rallies before you caught the competing bug, it is recommended that you go marshalling as your first *active* involvement with rallying. All rallies need marshals and it's an excellent way of getting the feel of the sport. If you haven't the initial confidence to tackle a control point by yourself, go along as an assistant. One thing is certain: the noise, the action and those marvellous smells of mud on hot exhaust systems and overworked brakes will certainly get you hooked on the sport.

It is obviously wise to decide at an early stage if you wish to concentrate on driving or navigating, although a dabble at both is an excellent thing before you get too serious. At this early stage, the potential driver need not have the latest specification of rally car. In fact, it's a positive *disadvantage* to possess such a vehicle for it could be dangerous if the capability of the car is way ahead of his skills. Better to start with a modest vehicle and work up to faster machinery.

Roger Clark started rallying in a Ford 5cwt Van whilst Russell Brookes drove an Austin Westminster before he graduated to a Morris Minor 1000 of his own. There are other stars, who used to borrow their company car for innocent events but we would not recommend this to anyone who hopes to get a gold watch for long service with their company!

The point we are making is that *any* type of car will be acceptable at these early stages and whatever the performance of the car you will soon see if you, as a driver or navigator, have any potential or any desire to progress to greater things.

A driver should simply see that the car is mechanically sound, has good underbody protection, good lights and tyres and, of course, good brakes. Obviously an experienced navigator can be an enormous help to a driver but it must be made quite clear that the driver is hoping to *learn* from his early events; he should not try to impress the experienced partner with great heroics.

Essential reading — the four 'blue books' covering all the rules, regulations and fixtures for motorsport Britain.

The navigator's beginning will be very similar to the driver's although *his* major investment will be a few pencils, one or two simple navigational instruments and an Ordnance Survey map or two. The problem of pairing is very much the same as the driver's — don't select a very experienced driver (if he'll have you) as you'll be so frightened of making a mistake that you will probably make one within a mile of the start.

Be completely honest with your partner and preferably learn together.

Many successful navigators started rallying at tender ages, among them Jim Porter and John Brown who began at seventeen. Mike Broad who navigated the winning car on the 1977 London-Sydney rally competed in his first event at fourteen. Some navigators start before they can drive a car and many do not even possess a car — we mention this because some people think that they cannot join a car club if they do not own a car. Not so! A navigator is fortunate because it will not cost a lot of money to practise.

Grasp every opportunity to compete on a rally, no matter how small. Practise map reference plotting and practise more difficult navigational exercises too. Get hold of old route cards from previous rallies and go through them. Then check them.

Some navigators have been known to sit in a darkened room in a rocking chair holding a torch, plotting map references under simulated rally car conditions. It's not a bad idea! If you can persuade a friend to take you for short drives, do so, and read the map whilst you go. You can follow a prescribed route from an old route card or even a route you have devised yourself. Try a few 'table top rallies' —motor clubs often run these as social evenings. Above all, gain every bit of experience you can — practise, practise, practise. Some top co-drivers have even been known to take Ordnance Survey maps to bed with them to practise plotting there! Other more normal beings might have better nocturnal activities in mind.

Whilst budding navigators are gaining as much map experience as possible, the driver should be concentrating on building up experience in the driving seat. Drive on as many events as you can. Don't worry if your car is unsuitable for the event in question, don't worry if you cannot win — just keep piling up those vital hours of experience. Loose surface auto-tests are always good and several clubs organise events of this nature. You may say that dodging plastic pylons is not what you aim to do for the rest of your motor sport career — don't worry, just think of the pylon as a fir tree or gatepost. There'll come a time when you'll be glad of that pylon dodging practice. Roger Clark competed regularly in auto-test meetings early in his career, although admittedly many of the major rallies of a few years ago used to conclude with tie-deciding driving tests.

Many top drivers have spent time gaining racing experience in their early careers while Stig Blomqvist, Per Eklund and John Taylor find rallycross good training for developing judgement, timing and car control.

Practise driving under all conditions. Don't go berserk racing around the lanes but do go for long drives on deserted tracks in adverse weather conditions. And if there is snow or fog — get out and practise. You'll be surprised how these two elements can alter rally results. Kyosti Hamalainen, one of the latest Finnish stars, practises every night of the week.

Many top drivers started driving at a very early age; some of those brought up in a motoring environment were capable drivers by the time they were ten years old! Needless to say, they only practised on private tracks or in fields.

Incidentally, it is surprising how many farmers' sons have become good rally drivers; Sandro Munari, Bjorn Waldegard, Andrew Cowan and Billy Coleman all cut their teeth on agricultural motoring. Timo Makinen once drove long distance lorries with trailers in snowy Lapland.

Whatever your background the message is clear: drive, drive, drive! Please do not trespass when practising your driving. **Do not,** ever, try to get onto Forestry Commission land or *any* private land; this will not only spoil your training plans if you are caught but, much more important, it will have a damaging effect on rally relations with land owners.

Remember that a good rally driver needs a combination of talents. He should have good balance, extremely good judgement, good reactions and good timing. The Americans have an apt saying to describe the cause of many motor sport accidents: "It was the right foot in the wrong place".

Speaking of balance, you may find motor cycle experience helpful. Tony Pond swears that it is his trail riding that helped him hone his driving skill. While German ace, Walter Rohrl was West German downhill ski champion and attributes his car control to that.

Although it is useful to try rallies with different partners, there is no doubt that you are likely to have more success if you develop a permanent partnership. It is important to develop a rapport with your partner particularly if you intend to compete in road rallies because the best road rally crews will almost be able to read each others' minds. A driver will understand instructions merely by the intonation in the navigator's voice when giving an instruction. Similarly, a navigator will be able to forestall a driver's question about the distance to petrol, or the penalty marks to date. A driver must be kept supplied with appropriate information (not too much trivia) although they do have an annoying habit of asking for it at the most inconvenient moments.

Even in stage rallies a good partnership is an advantage and when one starts to use pace notes the degree of trust and rapport which exists between the crew can be vital.

One of the problems encountered by the navigator in the early stages of map reading may be the dreaded travel sickness. Don't be put off by this rather unpleasant problem. Remember that most of today's top co-drivers have been sick at some time or another and travel sickness is usually overcome by confidence: confidence in your driver, confidence in your ability and confidence in your stomach. However, it will be wise to take one or two precautions at an early stage. Although some of the more experienced co-drivers eat copious supplies of fattening, filling food before an event (they work on the principle that they never know when it might be their last meal) it is wise to eat sensible amounts of *non-greasy* food before a rally. Naturally it would be irresponsible for either crew member to consider taking any alcohol. Don't starve yourself completely – you will not work accurately or efficiently if you are suffering from hunger pangs.

One of the major causes of travel sickness is the constant change in length of vision for the navigator – from the map to the road ahead and vice–versa. To avoid this, try to keep the knees which support the map-board as high as possible so that your eyes do not have to glance too far up or down when reading the map or when looking out of the windscreen – probably 50% of your time will be devoted to each. The other precaution is to have full harness seat belts **fastened as tightly as possible.** This keeps you at one with the car and although you might feel as though you are being shaken to pieces, you will find less of a sickness problem.

Finally, try proprietary brands of travel sickness pills. But experiment carefully – some of these have the side effect of making you drowsy.

If you really have a sickness problem and don't seem able to cure it, see your doctor, but make sure you tell him about your navigational role as some of the stronger travel drugs (only available on prescription) have a very strong drowsiness effect.

Both crew members should read as much about rallying as they can (there are lots of starving rally writers about – they all need your help). Go to rally film shows, listen and ask questions when your local club has an expert competitor as a guest speaker. Go to forums to listen and ask – you'll be surprised what you can learn. Even a fellow panellist learnt a new car control trick after listening to one of Timo Makinen's answers on a rally forum.

A driver can learn useful technical tips from lectures, forums and discussions, and he should certainly be reading as much as he can about rally preparation. Although some drivers are not particularly mechanically-minded, it is an advantage for the driver to have some mechanical knowledge.

A navigator usually has no interest whatsoever in the mechanics of a car, but it is again not a bad thing to have some basic knowledge. However your career develops and however many service crews you will employ, you'll still need to do your own running repairs from time to time.

Talking of service, you'll probably decide to take a service crew along when you do stage events (though only, repeat only, if permitted by the regulations). This may well be necessary if only to change wheels if you're lucky enough to have a choice of tyres. The service crew can fall into two categories – either a 'well equipped friend' (we're not talking about large ladies) or an estate car or van full of parts and tools. Either way, someone is going to have to pay.

Rallycross provides experience of driving on loose surfaces at high speeds.

Some club members will be delighted to pay their own petrol or hotel costs as it is their way of enjoying the sport – others may need a contribution. One thing is certain, you'll need to work out costs in detail and be very clear about who pays what long before the event. Good rally friendships have been ruined by financial misunderstandings.

Whilst on the topic of money we should also explain that there is no hard and fast rule for sharing expenses. Rallying is an expensive pastime, although the amount you spend depends on your level of participation. Basically, drivers are usually responsible for all the costs of car preparation, including parts, although it really depends on the personal financial situation of the competitors. It is not uncommon to share entry fees and running costs between navigator and driver, but on a stage event where the driver gains the greater kudos this may not be acceptable.

Whatever you decide, make sure it is cut and dried *before* you set off and also make sure who gets the prize money if any comes your way. However as this chapter is about the beginner in motor sport, it is unlikely you'll see much prize money at this stage.

It is necessary for the driver to be **absolutely sure his car is properly insured for any event** and whilst on the subject of insurance we should mention Life Insurance. Many policies exclude dangerous sports and for insurance purposes a rally is considered a dangerous sport. Some insurance companies can include an endorsement which allows rallying to take place, so make sure that yours is one – if not, change. Although we do not wish to become too macabre, a brief word about wills might not go amiss. As the events you enter grow in size, so will the distances you travel and there are, regrettably, occasional deaths involving travel and motor sports. See your Solicitor to make sure your affairs are in order.

5 Personal equipment

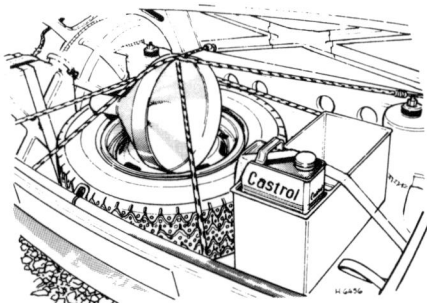

Safety and comfort are the two things to consider when choosing the first category of personal equipment — clothing.

Competitors on smaller road rallies will probably not need to go to the expense of purchasing overalls, but may simply wear slacks and pullover. Some drivers prefer 'shirt-sleeve order', others drive in a rally jacket with the car window open. Incidentally, drivers' window-opening habits should be borne in mind when navigators are planning *their* rallying wardrobe.

Footwear and gloves are again a matter of personal choice, but drivers' shoes should have no projections which might foul the pedals. Gloves should have chamois leather backs if you are likely to use them to clean the screen. Remember that whatever you wear, you're likely to find yourself scrambling under the car at some point so it's advisable not to wear your best suit.

A navigator on a road event may prefer to wear a jacket, or something with a few pockets, as a well organised individual will carry rubbers, spare pencils and other paraphernalia. He will also collect route-check cards and other bits of paper *en route*. Again, the latest Gucci footwear is not recommended for the navigator as he will probably find himself running along a ditch to a control at some time during a rally. Waterproof shoes are worth considering — in Canadian and Scandinavian winter rallies many co-drivers wear fur-lined boots with studded soles.

Rally overalls are now widely worn by drivers and navigators and they certainly make sense. Being purpose-built they save other clothing, keep the body at the right temperature, and may even make the crew feel and perform better. Fireproof overalls, whilst seldom compulsory in rallying, are popular. They are an undoubted safety precaution, although they can be a trifle uncomfortable on hot long-distance events.

Colour and design of overalls are matters of personal choice, although light colours are safer; you may find yourself dancing around in a forest track, or changing a wheel when another competitor comes along and you'll be seen more easily. Some overall manufacturers will only contemplate manufacturing one-piece suits. These are safer if the driver has to be pulled out of a car by outside helpers, although two-piece overalls seem more popular with rally crews.

Decorate your overalls with badges by all means, but try to keep a sense of neatness and decorum. Appearances are important and help the sport, so keep unnecessary and vulgar signs off your clothing. It's worth remembering that your most important decal (probably your sponsor's) should be as close to the chin as possible as this is the one seen on photographs and film and television interviews. Some people embroider their blood group on their overalls; a sensible safety precaution but professional crews will also have this on a wrist bracelet or on a disc round their neck as, in the unhappy event of an accident, their overalls might not reach hospital with them.

Rally jackets come in a proliferation of sizes, colours and designs and if you are not lucky enough to be given one by your team or sponsor then choose a practical one. As good a rule as any is to choose the type the works drivers wear. They are likely to be the right weight, be comfortable to wear and have pockets of the right size. Certainly the co-driver's jacket should have pockets large enough to carry passports, licences and rally documents like time-cards (the latter may have to be stored safely during waits at main rest halts or controls). Make sure the rally jacket has a built-in hood; many have fold away hoods and these are particularly suitable because there will be a cold, wet and windy night when you will welcome something to keep your head warm whilst waiting at a control or stage start (or when waiting for a breakdown truck!). Modern

Buy the best helmet you can afford. Russell Brookes shows the intercom fitted to his — the microphone is of soft-rubber and plastic designed to flex in an accident.

motoring fashions seem to have abandoned the time-honoured bobble-hat but you'll find that a cap or hat of some sort is useful if you need to leave the car in bad weather.

Talking of headwear brings us on to safety helmets — an essential part of rally equipment on all but the smallest road rally. When selecting a crash helmet make sure you choose one that fits you properly. **A badly fitting crash helmet can be more dangerous than no helmet at all.** In any case, unless you feel comfortable you will not be able to function in the rally properly. As a guide the following may be useful:

Crash helmet size chart

Size in inches (by tape measure)	$20\frac{1}{2}$	$20\frac{7}{8}$	$21\frac{1}{4}$	$21\frac{5}{8}$	22	$22\frac{1}{2}$	$22\frac{7}{8}$	$23\frac{1}{4}$	$23\frac{5}{8}$	24	$24\frac{3}{8}$
Hat size	$6\frac{3}{8}$	$6\frac{1}{2}$	$6\frac{5}{8}$	$6\frac{3}{4}$	$6\frac{7}{8}$	7	$7\frac{1}{8}$	$7\frac{1}{4}$	$7\frac{3}{8}$	$7\frac{1}{2}$	$7\frac{5}{8}$
Helmet size	Extra Small	Extra Small	S	S	M	M	L	L	Extra large	Extra large	Extra large

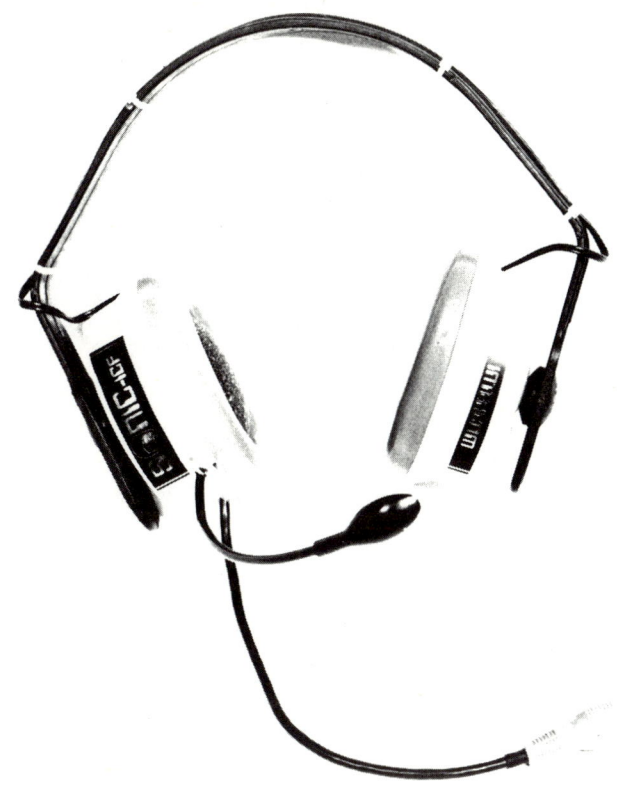

One half of an intercom set for road rallying.

Sizes in different makes may vary. Make sure the helmet you select is not too tight and certainly not too slack. A driver on one Manx Rally found that everything had gone dark after one particularly ferocious hump; his helmet was far too big and had slipped over his eyes. Not the safest way to go rallying!

Helmets are expensive but remember you are protecting a vital part of your body.

Decide whether you wish to wear a full-face or open-face model. There's a price difference and some people find a slightly claustrophobic effect when wearing a full face, but they are safe and find an increasing use in rallying today. In Italy and some other countries it is compulsory for both members of crew to wear full-face helmets.

Whatever style or make of helmet you select, make sure that your choice carries the latest British Standard numbers and therefore conforms to R.A.C. regulations. Helmets used in competition must conform to the following: British Standards 2495 (1960); British Standards 2495 (1977); Snell (USA) 1970, Snell (USA) 1975, not Z90. Helmets are — or should be — checked by the scrutineer before most major rallies and it is important that yours carries the approved number. Stickers to indicate that they are of an approved type have to be carried on helmets and these stickers are supplied by R.A.C. scrutineers. Make sure that the helmets are stored properly within the car. Do not throw helmets on the back seat after a stage as they are a confounded nuisance rolling around inside the rear of the car and, in any case, it doesn't do them much good.

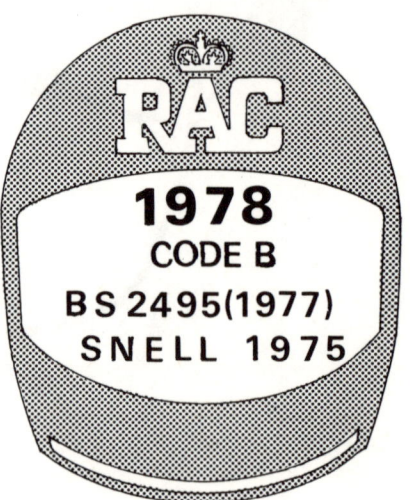

Crash hats must be checked by Scrutineers and carry these approved stickers. (Above, blue. Below, red).

Make a couple of boxes or brackets to carry the helmets but remember to position these so that you can reach them easily, preferably when wearing your seatbelts.

The engine noise inside a modern rally car is quite considerable and even worse when complemented by the sound of stones hitting the underside of the body. Therefore an intercom is desirable if the crew wish to communicate with each other clearly which, of course, they will when the co-driver is reading pace notes or route instructions to the driver. There must be no chance of an instruction being misunderstood so a good two-way intercom is essential. Not only will the driver wish to hear a co-driver's route instructions, he may also wish to *give* instructions during the course of the stage. Some drivers will ask their co-drivers to switch on the windscreen wipers, the auxiliary fuel pump, or flick a fuel tank switch during an event.

Having selected the intercom, make sure it is expertly fitted or is an integral part of the helmet; holes bored in a helmet weaken it and even nullify the British Standard Institute certificate. If your intercom has a boom mike make sure that this is flexible and made of a soft material, otherwise you may lose your front teeth in an accident.

Fitting the intercom in the car is important; it must be securely mounted. If fitted to the roll cage (the ideal place as it can be switched on and off easily) see that it can't drop off during bumpy going. Make sure that all electrical connections are good and regularly inspected and ensure that the leads from the helmet have simple jack-plug ends so that they can be pulled out easily.

One piece of 'equipment' which every crew member must carry is a competition licence. This takes the form of a club membership card for 'closed-to-club' rallies or an R.A.C. licence for other events. Licence fees and qualification requirements alter from time to time but, as a guide, these are the 1979 fees:

Drivers and co-drivers:

International	*£21.00*
National	*£11.00*
Restricted	*£ 6.00*
Temporary licence (valid for one week and only available for closed or restricted rallies)	*£ 4.00*

Food and drink are of absorbing interest to most rally drivers, consequently navigators will find it one of their chores to 'feed and water' their drivers regularly. Although the days of picnic hampers laden with chicken legs and champagne have passed by, it is necessary to carry a few tit-bits in a rally car because sensible food and drink can refresh a crew when its energy is waning.

Sandwiches and items that deteriorate are not a good idea nor are messy, crumbly or intricately wrapped foods. Most works drivers carry a small supply of boiled sweets, Polo mints, glucose tablets, chewing gum and possibly apples. Cheese can fall into the 'messy' category but a number of drivers swear by it.

Take a bottle of orange squash, lemonade, glucose drink or mineral water but keep it tightly secured within the car and avoid very 'gassy' mineral waters as they are likely to cascade all over your car when the tops are removed.

A cup of hot coffee is an excellent reviver in the middle of the night but vacuum flasks seldom survive more than one rally so you may either rely on cafes kept open for controls by organisers or leave the supply of coffee to your service crew. Although the role of the service crew is dealt with in a later chapter, it is worth mentioning that a good service crew will always provide food and drink for its drivers. Works crews may enjoy soup, coffee, sandwiches, cheese, yoghurts, biscuits or whatever specialities they desire. 'Reg' Redgewell of the Ford Service Team produces such gastronomic delights that it was once rumoured that his Transit was up for an Egon Ronay Award! Opel's famous service bus has its own *Cordon Bleu* cook on board. Mechanic Norman Masters, whilst not achieving such dizzy heights of *haute cuisine* always provides a good selection of biscuits and cakes and in order to test Roger Clark's insatiable appetite once provided a plate of dog biscuits. Clark was halfway through when he was told what they were; he merely said 'how nice' and finished the lot.

Never be afraid or embarrassed about carrying personal items in the car. Some drivers carry a set of goggles in case the windscreen pops out, some carry a knife, a crowbar, sunglasses (very important), spare socks or a spare ignition key fastened to the zip of their rally jacket. You'd be surprised how many rally crews have incurred time penalties when they couldn't unlock their car after a control because they'd lost the ignition key!

Finally, if you have a lucky charm and think it makes you drive better then by all means carry it—confidence is half the battle and you'll need all the luck you can get anyway.

A selection of competition licences. They must be signed and carry a photograph of the holder to be valid.

6 Car preparation

Having sorted out your personal preparation we can now consider the car. First a word of caution: don't put a spanner anywhere near a rally car until you have squarely faced up to one or two questions:

How much can you afford to spend? A lot of rally programmes fizzle out part way through because the crew forgot to work out a proper budget.

What type of rallies are you proposing to enter? There is no point in spending money to build a car like a tank if you are going to concentrate on smooth, tarmac rallies.

Are you really certain that you are Britain's answer to the Scandinavians? Really sure? Because if you aren't then it doesn't make sense to build a full-blooded — and very, very expensive — works replica. Far too many people waste money preparing cars which are way ahead of their driving ability.

So, having done our best to disillusion you, let us now move on to discuss just how to prepare your rally car.

Study the regulations. Simple to say but from the clangers people drop it would seem to be difficult to do.

Study the regulations for your type of rallying and study the homologation form for your car until you are quite sure you know exactly what you are allowed to do. In particular it is unforgivable to be caught cheating in one of the 'one-make' rally championships. Experience has shown that in those the odd 2 or 3bhp doesn't make a blind bit of difference so it just isn't worth sailing close to the edge of the regulations to gain them.

Remember that if your car is new then virtually anything you do to it for motor sport will clobber your warranty!

Before you start work, try to talk to one or two people running the same make of car—they should be able to alert you to any pitfalls.

Do you have any mechanical skill? If not, but can find a friend to help you work on the car, then it is worth tackling your own preparation. At one time the works teams were happiest with drivers with little mechanical knowledge; not so nowadays when testing and general sorting is so important in rallying—just as it is in Formula 1. If you do your own work on your rally car you will be more capable of fixing it during an event.

What workshop space do you have? Marriages have been broken by engine rebuilds under the bed. Remember that a stripped rally car can take up a lot of space. And *if* you have the time and money that is how you should start: by stripping your car down to the shell. *Not* essential of course, and you may win rallies just by bolting on a couple of extra lights, but you will be absolutely *sure* of your car if it has had a total rebuild.

This is the time to fit wheel-arch extensions and do any other welding or cutting and shutting—such as putting a fireproof bulkhead behind the rear seats.

Whatever your budget limitations, you must not cut corners on safety items.

So now fit an interior roll cage and make it a full-house version with tubes down the windscreen pillars. Pad the cage with rubber and cover any protruding bolts.

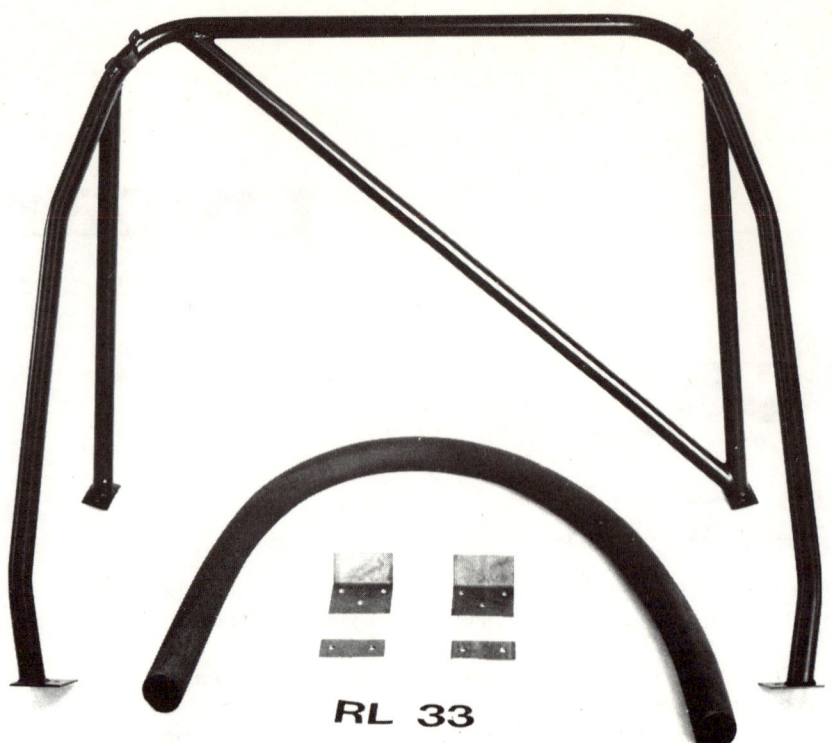

*A good roll-over
bar is essential.*

While you have the car stripped down, do what you can to block off holes so that the car stays fairly free from dust and water during a rally.

Next, the area which loses more rallies than anything else: the electrics. Sit quietly with a large sheet of paper and *plan* what is going to go where on your car and sort out your wiring accordingly. Always use the correct specification of wire for a particular load and obviously vary the colours so that you can identify things.

Don't ramble wires around the car; keep things as neat and tidy as possible. Use grommets wherever necessary and avoid sharp edges. The list goes on: connections need to be grease free and tight; battery terminals should be kept clean; fuseboxes should be accessible: fit relays to the horn and extra lamps to reduce the voltage drop. In other words *attention to detail*.

You may well decide to uprate the alternator; if so, make sure you fit the correct bracket etc, because this is a vulnerable area. If you *do* change the alternator don't forget to have the control box and regulator checked to suit the power and the battery—over-charging can be nearly as big a headache as undercharging.

If your wife or girl friend hasn't strangled you with a jump lead by now and you have a car with impeccable wiring, start putting the suspension back so that you can get the car onto its wheels. Don't start experimenting with suspensions, fit whatever the leading drivers use who run your type of car. It is too early in your career to get neurotic over suspension settings.

Use heavy duty bushes where available and fit a high ratio steering rack; don't underestimate the arm effort needed for modern high speed rallying.

Moving to the other end of the car, install the best axle you can afford (we appreciate this implies a front engined, rear wheel driven car—this is because most current rally winners have this configuration). Drivers always want low ratios, team managers like to play safe with high. The drivers are usually proved right!

Make very sure that the bump stops work before the shock absorbers are fully compressed, otherwise you will damage the brackets or, worse, the turrets.

Spring rates and ride heights will be controlled to some extent by the type of rallies you are doing; as a general rule attempts to jack-up cars into the sky cause all sorts of other problems and aren't successful. Anyway you will be protecting your engine with one of the most important fittings: a sump guard. Get a good one and fit it properly. If you fit an expensive lightweight sump guard add a sheet of thin mild steel to it—it will be cheaper to replace this now and again than buy a new guard.

We nearly forget: fit a limited slip diff of course but *only* if it is allowed under the regulations. It is a very easy thing for a scrutineer to check!

The roll-over bar should be padded to protect the crew in an accident. Note the flexible map light mounted to the bar.

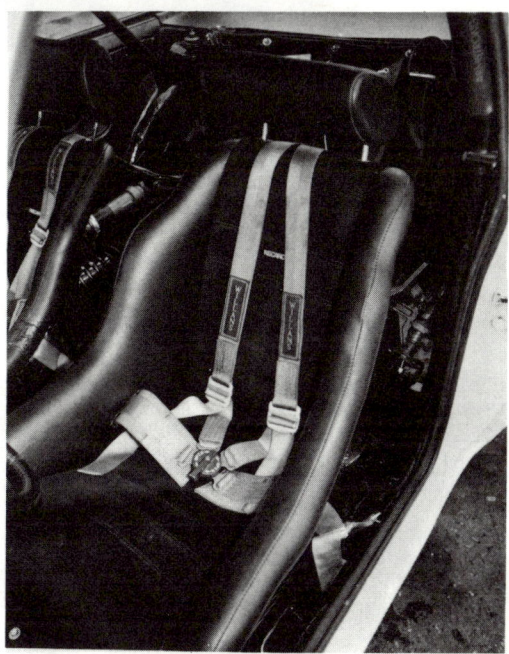

Mount the seats firmly and fit full safety harnesses.

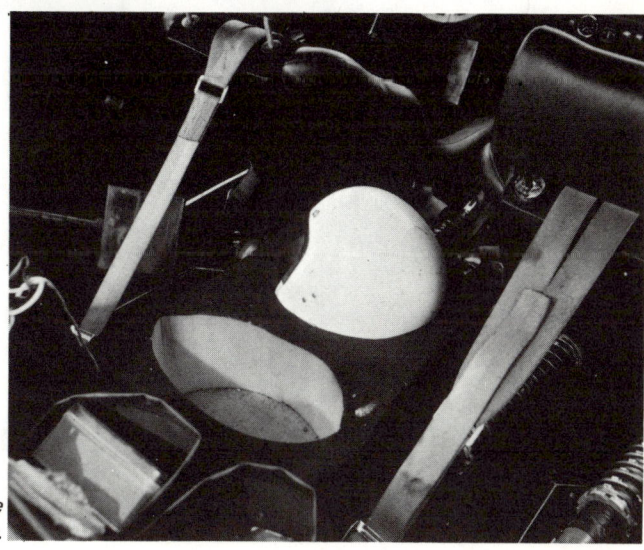

Fit some form of crash hat carrier — like this made from a slab of foam.

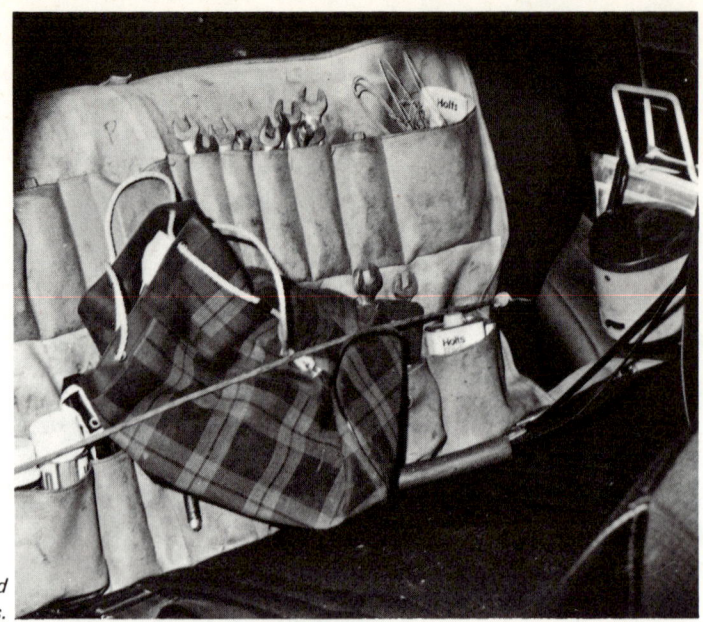

A pouch on the back seat makes a good home for spanners and spares.

The interior should look neat – like this TR7. Note the extra pockets in front of the co-driver.

If the cost of all this is starting to frighten you, bear in mind that if you are an undiscovered genius then you may be able to shine in your aunt's old shopping car, but it is unlikely. You just have to accept that motor sport of any sort is going to cost you money!

So let us spend some more of your money and consider the clutch. Most standard clutches have a certain safety margin—say 10% or so—so if you are leaving your engine standard your clutch should cope. Better though to fit a competition one. Considering how much more reliable they make rally cars, competition clutches are quite cheap and are usually interchangeable with the standard ones.

Having taken some trouble with your axle (such as by having the best available halfshafts) and fitted a competition clutch, now get your propshaft properly balanced before fitting it.

Remember what we said about not economising on safety? Well, here we go again because the next item to consider is the brakes. Brake pipes must be well protected and run inside the car where possible. The flexible hoses should have protective springs coiled round them. Washers and seals should be replaced regularly—an advantage of doing your own maintenance and preparation is that you will get a feel for when this should be. Discs and drums must be running true, wheel bearings must be checked regularly, drums should be cleaned out regularly and you need competition brake fluid. All obvious things, but all important.

If you have a dual-line braking system with one cylinder operating the front brakes and another the rear you will, if the cylinders have an adjustable swinging beam between them, be able to 'tune' the balance of the braking between front and rear. *But*, ladies and gentlemen, this is for experts—don't waste time or money on such sophistication until you are very, very sure that you are capable of making use of it.

Be neat in the boot too. Make sure the spare wheel cannot bounce about.

The engine compartment must be given maximum attention.

Having spent money on the engine, protect it with a good sump guard.

With only mild power increases you should be able to stop OK if you simply fit competition brake material. Bed the pads and/or shoes in as advised by the manufacturer and if you expect to have to change during an event, bed a spare set in beforehand. If a material change isn't enough to give you proper stopping power then **consult an expert** before you venture into a complete system change—we don't want to lose you (we need someone to buy our next book)!

Modify the handbrake to give it a fly-off action.

Wheels? Well a lot of people get carried away by cosmetics and fit wheels which may be prettier but are in fact heavier than standard, which is silly. Simple advice: follow the advice of people who are winning in your car. Don't go overboard on rim widths.

Happily some of the one-make rally championships are stipulating one type of tyre. Sensible, because tyre permutations and costs have done more damage to rallying than perhaps we realise. When you hear works teams talk of 600 tyres for a three car team on a Monte and £20,000 for tyres for a Swedish Rally for a two car team, perhaps it is time for a still, small voice to cry "enough"?

Because of the competition between manufacturers—which can only benefit the clubman—it would be dangerous in this book to give advice on particular tyres because things change quickly. Our only advice is not to burden yourself with the cost of umpteen tyre permutations until your driving deserves them. Once again—ask the leading competitors for advice but this time probe them on the puncture record of particular tyres—in your early stages you want to have trouble free rallies while you shake yourself down; you won't get them if you are constantly changing wheels because of punctures.

Anyway, now you should have a well prepared shell, fitted with a sump guard and safety cage and with a well sorted axle, prop-shaft, gearbox, etc, (we will come to the engine later). And presumably at some stage you will have had the car painted. Although rallying has improved its image over the years with the growth of sponsorship, there are still very few cars *properly* presented with eye catching colour schemes—and the works are as guilty as anyone else. Give it some thought and if you or a mate have got styling flair you may attract attention simply because you have a well presented car. Remember too that the cleaner and crisper your car looks, the better ride you may have with scrutineers.

Axles are vulnerable – note the bracing bar and skid plate fitted to this one.

Now let us move inside the car. Seats are a matter for personal preference. They should be strong and firmly bolted down with zero play. The fore and aft position should be tailored for the number one driver.

Back to safety, fit the best seat belts you can get and **fit them properly.** You will be bounced about a lot on special stages so you must be able to strap yourself in firmly. The co-driver will probably want to sit well back in the car (out of your way as you do your Hero Driver bit) in which case a bracing bar for his feet will be necessary so that he can push himself into his seat as he sits there counting his beads.

When did you last have an instrument fail in a standard car? Probably never. Which is a good argument for not loading your rally car with a battery of extra dials. You should have an oil gauge or warning light of course; adjust it so that you get a warning *before* any damage is done.

The co-driver will need a plug for his light which brings us into the realm of ergonomics (the word adds a touch of culture to the book if nothing else). Get with your co-driver and sit in the car and then decide where you are going to place his plug, any auxiliary switches, a torch holder, crash hat supports and so on. Don't mount extra switches in groups of more than three—there is a limit to how far most drivers can count.

Additional lights sometimes fall into the area of machismo. Fit what you are allowed; fit the best; mount them so that they won't wobble about; wire them properly—then forget them. Don't blame the lights if you get murdered on every night stage, find out first if you are one of those people who simply hasn't got very good night vision. Make sure additional lights comply with the law.

Skids on the silencer will help to protect it from damage. Adequate silencing is essential if rallying is to avoid antagonising the public.

Spot lamps flapping about do not give a driver confidence. Note the adjusting/supporting bar at the top of this one.

Incidentally, if you are serious about saving weight (and you should be) you could perhaps have quick release plugs for auxiliary lights so that they can be removed on daylight sections (provided the regulations allow this) and carried in a support car. Only do this if it can be organised without any hassle.

Back to our ergonomics, neatness must be the watchword. Stow everything safely and carry this theory back to the boot too. Don't allow a heavy spare wheel to fly about, nor a battery for that matter which can be even more dangerous. If your boot needs a key to open it, wire one in place during a rally to save time. A safety bag petrol tank is nice to have, though costly of course. Locking petrol caps should be replaced before a rally—they waste time.

You must naturally have a fire extinguisher on board and the car must have a clearly marked external switch for the electrical circuit so that a spectator can operate it if, for instance, you are trapped in a car after a shunt.

You will need a tow rope. Oh yes you will. If you leave the back seat out you can replace it with a canvas or plastic sheet with stowage pockets and carry the tow rope in there—along with spare wiper blades, tyre levers and (for events a fair way from home) a spare gasket set.

With all the weight you have added there is something to be said for leaving the carpets at home. The car will be noisier but will be as noisy as hell anyway with stones being hurled about underneath on forest stages. Having saved that weight, put a bit back by carrying a first aid kit.

Rubber flaps like this help keep the lights and screen clear.

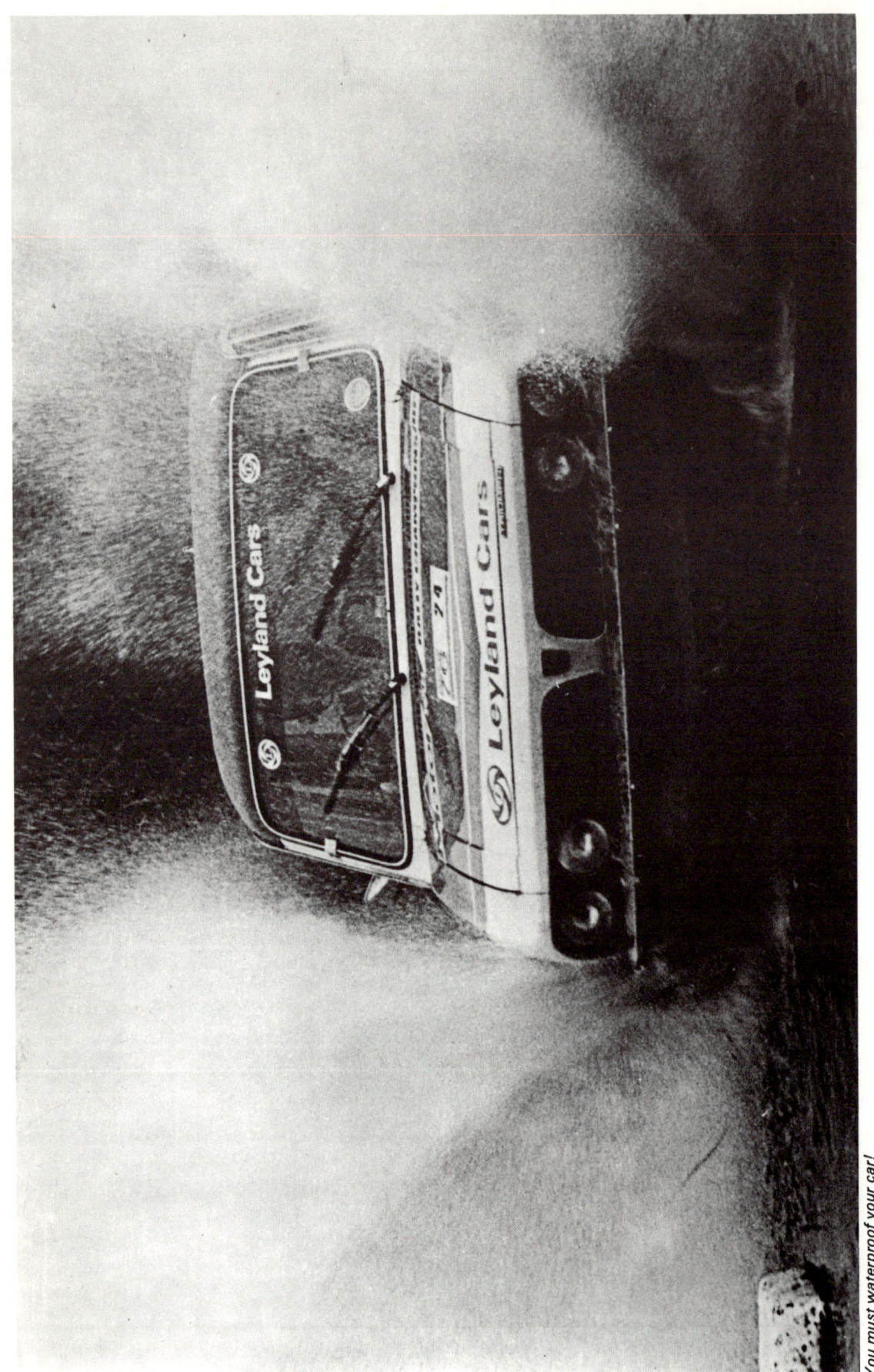

You must waterproof your car!

Cars should always be clean at scrutineering – particularly if you have a car polish manufacturer as sponsor!

Nearly finished the preparation saga now, but there is still one thing to consider—the engine. As we mentioned earlier, Eric Carlsson made as big an impact on rallying in his day as anyone else and he weighed 18 stone and his Saab had a tiny engine. In the old Mexico championship whenever Peter Ashcroft put a few cars on a rolling road he often found the winners were a few bhp down on the rest. As we never tire of repeating on forums, if it is dark, cold and wet and you are going downhill on a loose surface then power to weight is less important than driving ability, far less; which is a long winded way of saying don't waste money on engine tuning until your driving is up to it.

A basic but worthwhile improvement can be gained by simply stripping the engine and having it rebuilt under what is picturesquely called "blueprinting", in other words getting everything to the best tolerance for performance. Combustion chambers can be balanced and equalised; manifolds and ports can be matched precisely and so on. Probably more trouble than it is worth for average rallying—more relevant to production car racing perhaps, but if you do it you may *feel* the car is quicker and have more confidence as a result (and confidence is half the battle) and at least the stripping and rebuilding will give you an intimate knowledge of your engine.

If you get involved in more elaborate engine tuning we recommend that you aim for mid-range torque rather than out and out top-end performance. It may be impressive at the bar to casually mention a high bhp figure but if it is only achieved at very high revs (and your gearing means that you only reach it after seven miles flat-out on Pendine Sands) it won't exactly do you much good on plod and bash rallies. But then not too many rallies are won at the bar nowadays, otherwise the results tables would be vastly different.

The key phrase under more general tuning is "machining and polishing" because if the regulations permit you can clearly improve engine performance by raising compression and generally improving the gas flow. In this category valves, pistons, springs and so on will be free but—and we hate to keep preaching but we *are* trying to save you money—go for reliability and when possible copy the experts (and in your case an 'expert' should be regarded as someone who finishes fairly well up regularly i.e., with a reliable car).

Rallying has its opponents and noise is quoted as one of the sport's most irritating features so fit a good exhaust system and make sure it will stay in place. You have decided to take up rallying so that you can have a roarty car to impress the birds? Well, we admire your rather muddled motives but could you possibly clear-off and take up another sport?

Even a standard exhaust manifold will have a longer life if you strengthen it with a support bracket taken off the bellhousing: you should also tack weld all the joints in the system to keep it in one piece. Add 'skids' of mild steel strip to each end of the silencer box—as well as at any other vulnerable points—to stop the box being knocked off on rocks. Sooner or later you will have to reverse in a fairly narrow space, if your exhaust pipe sticks out at the back it will get filled with earth. Keep it short.

The early rally pictures in this book featured no sponsors' advertising. All that has changed! Lamp covers are a 'high exposure' area ...

... as is the boot lid. Note the mud flaps rolled up strapped out of the way.

Prime advertising sites are below the front bumper ...

... or along the top of the screen.

Switches for the battery mains and fire extinguisher must be readily accessible outside the car in case the crew are trapped in an accident.

In theory the car should now be nearly ready for its first event. But pause. Go over the car carefully.

Any bolts sticking out where they can catch against a pipe or wire? Any bolts sticking out which could catch against *you* if you roll over? Any brackets which you bodged-up in a hurry and which spoil the overall look of the car? Remake them.

Jack, tools, wheelbrace, first aid kit, sweeties all carefully stowed? Sponsor's stickers neatly displayed? Can you get full throttle?

When you are satisfied on all these things take your baby out, grit your teeth and drive it in anger over a local rough road. Go on, force yourself. If it won't survive a couple of miles of this, how do you expect it to survive a rally?

Often things which are going to come loose will do so in the first couple of miles—better that these are test miles, rather than on an actual event. When you get back from the test run, check everything again, then wash and polish the car before you report to the start of a rally. All sports are getting more professional in their presentation—even darts and snooker—so don't let motor sport down by appearing in something that looks as if it has escaped from a banger race.

Some events allow service. Many argue against it—including at times the works teams who are horrified at the cost of helicopters and planes on Safaris and such like.

If you are on a rally and works teams are present *don't* expect the works mechanics to mother you. They will have different priorities. In fact the only real way to grab their attention is to go so well that you end up beating the works cars. But it ain't easy.

If you put out your own service car *please* do not set it high average speeds between service points. Too many mechanics have had accidents that way.

A service car should have adequate springs to cope with the load of parts and of course the brakes should be in perfect condition. Don't carry parts which will take hours to fit; make do and mend items make more sense. Rope and a large hammer are essentials! Have a check-list for the service car so that you don't forget anything.

7 Rally driving

Have you had a medical check recently? Are your eyes O.K.? If you wear glasses have you had them checked lately?

All points worth considering before you try to become a rally driver. Not much point in spending a lot of money on extra lights if your eyes need testing. Not much point in shaving a few grams off the weight of your car if you've got a bulbous belly.

Don't get us wrong—you don't have to be a superman to do well on rallies and certainly you don't have to be as fit as say, a marathon runner or sprinter. But consider for a moment ... The standard of competition is high so doesn't it make sense to get yourself in the best possible shape before you start rallying?

If nothing else, if you are fit you will be better able to push your car out of a forest if you have a breakdown.

One other thing before you start rally driving. Have you been to one of the rally schools? Worth doing because although you may have to lay out £50 or so, it is better to do this rather than spend a lot more on preparing a car only to find that you have little or no basic aptitude. If you make this unhappy discovery but decide to plough on, at least the knowledge can steer you in the right direction on cars and preparation.

One rather important benefit of a rally school is that it will give you a chance to sit with a star driver and study his technique.

Having decided to continue, you now need to get yourself into gear—overalls, crash hat, gloves, shoes and so on. No need to go berserk on your equipment at the beginning but let us repeat what we said in an earlier chapter: make sure clothing is practical and comfortable. Don't wear anything for the first time on an event; if your new fireproof underpants choke you (you may have your own priorities on what you want to protect) find out before, not on, a rally. We made the point in car preparation that the sport needs smart presentation so please don't turn up at the start of a rally in greasy, torn overalls. Keep an old pair for working on the car, a better pair for driving in.

Medical experts reckon that it takes up to thirty minutes for your eyes to adjust to darkness after being in bright lights ... So carry sunglasses to put on at night controls, where there may be TV lights and photographers' flash guns. Obviously you will also need the sunglasses on bright days. Night driving glasses are not recommended.

Once you have kitted yourself out with proper clothing and equipment, you need to blend yourself with your car. Can you reach all the controls when you are strapped in? Are you happy with the pedals? Is the seat mounted properly for you? Most drivers seem happier with more of a sit-up-and-beg driving position than that adopted by racing drivers—it obviously helps to be able to see enough to 'place' a car. Don't have the seat ludicrously high of course, otherwise you will end up as the Hunchback of Notty Ash!

If you like a steering wheel with a turquoise, sheepskin cover then fit it, duckie, but don't expect it to make you any quicker. There is really not much wrong with standard steering wheels but if you feel happier with something different—be our guest.

Remember that a steering wheel is not intended as an additional grab handle, just for steering.

Don't bother too much with fine tuning the suspension and brakes until you have a little experience, nor should you become obsessive about tyre pressures.

You may have your own views on how you want to set your lights—clearly they mustn't irritate non-competing cars coming the other way—do remember to set the lights with car fully laden *in rally trim.*

That means with your co-driver onboard. This poor devil is the guy who can rarely win a rally for you,

Perhaps rally drivers don't need to be as fit as race drivers but it helps. Ari Vatanen cycles to keep fit.

but he can certainly lose one, so choose him/her with care. In fact in your early days it is worth doing a rally or two as a navigator yourself, this will give you some idea of the problems the co-driver faces and therefore the qualities you need to look for in one. If you are totally without experience then you are not going to get the star co-drivers leaping into your car so you will just have to look for someone who is pleasant to get on with and, hopefully, a disciplined thinker and good at figures. Note that "pleasant to get on with" is listed first. Let's face it: rallying is a sport which should be done for fun—why put up with a miserable sod just because he is a good co-driver?

Can your proposed co-driver drive? Will you be able to rest while he steers you from one special stage to another? Has he driving ambitions of his own? (if so turn through 180 degrees and run away as fast as you can).

Can he/does he write for any of the motoring papers? If so it may help you to get assistance from overseas rallies which may be glad of media coverage.

Now you have sorted out yourself and your car and found a co-driver, don't set off for a rally just yet. Practise first.

Go out over local roads (at night) and shake yourself down as a crew. Get used to each other's language (it may get colourful under stress). Practise wheel changing; few crews do but it can save vital seconds on a stage if you know where everything is stowed and who is going to do what during the wheel change. And practise wearing full rally gear including crash hats!

Watch some of the top works pairings in action—or for that matter the more professional road rally crews like Bill Gwynn and Terry Thorp—and you'll begin to appreciate what the sport is about.

By this stage you should have enough confidence to concentrate on how to become a better driver, safe in the knowledge that you have taken care as far as possible of all the factors contributing to success—the car, co-driver, etc.

And if you want to become a star driver (or simply a competent clubman) then it sounds obvious but as we said earlier there is one thing you must do above all else and that is *drive*. Drive everything and anything at every opportunity. Hannu Mikkola had a season of saloon car racing based on Rochdale (very character forming) and it put an edge on his driving. We are not suggesting you need a full season of club racing but certainly a few races will give you a wider appreciation of speed. Autotests, rallycross, autocross-anything; if it has four wheels and an engine, then drive it.

Keep records. In other words log all the events you do, making a note of other competitors and how you fared against them (so that you can see if you are improving if you meet them later). Log where you finished, how many starters, how well the event was run, any marshalling problems, any difficulty in getting hotels, any problems in finding the start, and so on and so on and so on. The sort of thing which will help you to do better on the rally the following year.

There is something to be said for a season or so of *road* events before you tackle the tougher stage rallies—it will certainly bed you in as a crew. When you do get onto stage events you will quickly realise the obvious: rallies are won or lost on corners. Given the right sized wellie anyone can drive fast in a straight line. You must learn to corner well.

The technique is obviously governed by the road surface. If you are on dry tarmac then the neatness of a racing driver is appropriate. Incidentally, note how most of the sideways Formula One men eventually settle down to a more controlled line. And a smooth line is particularly important with the lower-powered one-make championships—hurl the car about too much and you will scrub off all your speed!

The Circle Exercise

NOTE THE VARYING POSITIONS OF THE CAR RELATIVE TO THE CIRCLE AND THE FRONT WHEELS TO THE CAR.

THE AIM IS TO TRAVEL AROUND THE CIRCLE OF BOLLARDS AT A CONSTANT THROTTLE WITH THE CAR IN AN OVERSTEERING ATTITUDE - BALANCING THE CAR WITH SLIGHT MOVEMENTS OF THE STEERING WHEEL.

IT'S NOT SO EASY AS IT LOOKS!

A page from the Ford Rally School Handbook. The circle exercise may seem elementary but as the book says it is NOT as easy as it looks. Try it on a loose surface. If nothing else it will teach you that rally driving can be hard work.

But even if the road is dry and the sun is shining and the birds are singing you must cultivate one thing: *determination.*

You must want to win. You must want to will the blasted car to the end of the stage. You must shut your mind to anything but that one objective, getting the car to the finish as fast as possible.

Experience at the Ford Rally School indicates that people just will not *concentrate.* The same with the Find-a-Lady-Driver programme Ford ran. All the star drivers who acted as judges commented that well over half the girls were happy to tour round or to gaze at the crowd. The girls who got anywhere were the ones who said the hell with anything other than pressing the car to its limit.

If you concentrated when on tarmac, you will have to concentrate just as hard on loose surfaces. If you are enough of an enthusiast to have bought this book and waded this far you will probably have seen one of the excellent rally films there are about. If so you will have noticed one thing: cars don't go round corners in a conventional fashion. The back ends of the cars are swinging this way and that.

This is because if you drive round a loose corner in the conventional way, as you speed up you will understeer off the road. Note when the first ice of winter hits the country how many people slide off into ditches on the outside of bends; in other words they have understeered off. The same thing will happen on a loose special stage unless you set up the car to stop it. Purists may argue that you could tune suspensions to remove the understeer but they forget that the surfaces are loose and sometimes rough, which tends to clobber theory.

If you are approaching a left-hand bend on a loose surface and deliberately put the car into an unstable situation by a sharp turn on the steering wheel to the right, you will then be able to flick or 'pendulum' the car back round to the left to go round the corner and because of the controlled (at least we hope it is controlled) instability you will avoid going off through understeer. It may look like one long accident looking for somewhere to happen when you see it for the first time, but it really is safer and faster. Obviously humps and bumps may throw you off your intended line in the middle of a corner so you must be ready to correct immediately.

The ability to have a car under control on a loose surface is the key to success on special stages. At the rally schools you will find yourself asked to drive round and round a single pylon—holding the car on line with throttle control. John Taylor's party trick at the Ford Rally School is to stand like a matador with perspiring pupils going round and round him in a tight circle.

This not only teaches car control—it makes people realise that you have to work hard and concentrate. Their beaming grins quickly fade when they realise they really have to put some effort into it and *concentrate*.

If all else fails and a slide off the road seems inevitable you still have one friend left: the handbrake. If you are doing 25mph or so, then yank on the steering wheel and at the same time de-clutch and tug at the handbrake (which should be the fly-off type) you will find, to your co-driver's surprise (and possibly yours) that you have turned through 180 degrees. And it can be done in roads only slightly wider than the car is long. Both authors during misspent youths as navigators have overshot turnings and been pivoted through 180 degrees by drivers doing handbrake turns.

Don't practise it on public roads. Find somewhere quiet and loose and keep doing it until you can judge the right amount of effort and sharpness to put into your actions. Once you have mastered it you can use the technique to spin to a stop if you are in danger of going off and, with practise, you will be able to use the handbrake to induce the instability we talked about and hence help your general cornering particularly on hairpins. Caution though—don't get neurotic about it, concentrate on your general driving technique first.

And the same applies to the dreaded left-foot braking, which mainly applies to front-wheel-drive cars. It is a much discussed technique and can work well *with the right talent* but it should be a long way down your list of things to learn.

The pedals must be adjusted until the driver is completely happy with them. Note the support for the left foot – don't use the clutch as a resting place!

This Dunlop MS564 tyre carries 600 studs and would be used on pure snow and ice. However, more and more organisers now ban studded tyres.

A selection of Dunlop rally tyres. Brief descriptions, starting Top Left.

CR82	Intermediate race-rally tyres specially designed for Group 1 cars' use on tarmac stages.
CR65	Another intermediate pattern and compound for use on tarmac stages by 2-litre, Group 1 or 1600cc Group 2 cars.
CR82	Same construction for use on powerful Group 4 cars with 7 inch or 8 inch width wheels.
SP SUPER	High speed radial particularly suitable for road rallies.
SPR3	Specially designed for 'clubmen' – a compromise for stage and road use.
A2 'M&S'	A forest tyre for dry, smooth stages.

Bottom row Left to Right:

MS	A 12 inch forest tyre made by Dunlop, Japan.
MS	13 inch version extensively used by Group 1 cars.
MS Mk II	Popular tyre for rough, muddy stages. This 6 inch version is used on front wheels.
MS Mk II	Rear wheel tyre 7 inch width.
MS SNOW	A winter tyre for use when studs are banned.
MS564	Another effective snow tyre developed in Finland (also used to good effect in autocross, grass track racing or very muddy rallycross).
MS SNOW	15 inch version specially developed for SAAB team winter rallies.
MS 'E'	A development of the old SP44 rally tyre. A cheaper compromise tyre for use by clubmen.

The big problem with front wheel drive cars when driven in anger is that as you apply the power the front wheels may loose their grip, which in turn induces understeer, which can be terminal if you don't do something about it. The Scandinavians worked out that if you keep your right foot on the accelerator and put your left foot on the brake you can control the rear wheels through the braking system, while your right foot (and hopefully the steering too of course) controls the front end. Using the left-foot on the brakes makes the back end come round, just as the handbrake does. For the same reason most drivers have their brakes biased towards the rear.

The brakes being on while the accelerator is pressed can also act as something of a limited slip, although if you are too enthusiastic with the left-foot you will simply slow yourself down.

Bear in mind that unless you are very careful you will burn out your brakes and be no quicker, so let us repeat: only try it when you have explored and mastered the other techniques. Try to see the old Castrol film of the Flying Finns which features Timo Makinen demonstrating the technique in a Mini. He makes it quite clear that you have to change gear without using the clutch, which may be less than appealing if you are buying your own gearboxes!

In theory you can use the same left foot technique on front engined, rear-wheel-drive cars but it must be stressed that more rallies are won without using it. The idea is that it helps you to balance a car better and that in particular it can help you to take off properly before a brow so that you 'fly' at the right angle.

Incidentally if a brow is 'blind' try not to approach it in a straight line. The Scandinavians work on the reasonable theory that if someone has taken the trouble to build a road through a forest and up a hill, then presumably they have continued the road on the other side of the hill *but* (and there so often is a 'but' in rallying) there may be a T-junction just the other side. If you fly majestically over the brow pointing straight ahead, you may well exit from the rally through the fence which is also straight ahead.

If you come over with the car slightly out of line (in the unstable position we talked about earlier) then you will be better placed to flick the car round the corner.

We are all happy that all this is taking place on roads closed to other traffic aren't we … ? Good.

If you wake up one morning and the roads are covered in snow, don't go back to bed. Get out and practise.

We see snow so rarely in Britain that it makes sense to use every opportunity to get the feel of driving on it. You will need to use similar techniques to driving on the loose and the same applies to sheet ice of course. Note by the way that under slippery conditions, top drivers will de-clutch if all is lost. By removing the drive from the wheels it makes things as smooth as possible and may keep you in control of the situation. Practise this if possible.

On a rally in snow your running order is critical, as is the track of your car. If you have a different track to everyone else you may find yourself having to master virgin snow all the time. By the way Scandinavians tend to favour narrow tyres on snow.

For known snowy conditions you may on some events be allowed to use studded tyres. Our advice? Ask Dunlops if they have any good secondhand studded tyres left over from previous years and use those. The top drivers will sometimes get into a sweat over this make of stud or that type of bonding—just as skiers argue over the best type of preparation for their skis–but when the chips or flakes are down it all hinges on how quick the driver is.

What else? Oh yes. Fog! Horrid stuff but you will meet it sooner or later. No known technique for seeing through it. If someone passes you, try to hang on to them, at the risk of following the District Nurse into her drive.

In Formula One it seems to be an accepted tactic to make it difficult for another driver to get past. Not so in rallying. If someone catches you up it means they are quicker than you are, so get out of the way as soon as you can. *Never* baulk other cars.

It is a few pages since we last mentioned it so let us remind you again: *concentrate*. Concentrate in fog. Concentrate in rain and don't forget to concentrate on *easy* road sections. If you are chatting about your heroic performance on the last stage some of the shine will be taken off if you hit the back of a milk-float through not paying attention.

In the split of duties the driver should really be the one in touch with the mechanical needs of the car so as you are running into a fuel stop, control or overnight halt, dictate a list of 'jobs to be done' to the co-driver. And try to prioritise things. The fact that your jelly-baby holder has come loose is slightly less important than that the exhaust is falling off. If, sadly, you are faced with a major job—such as a gearbox change—the co-driver should be working out exactly how much time will be in hand both before and *after* the stop, while you think through how to tackle the job.

With experience you should be able to pace yourself. We say "should" although this does seem to take some of the young Scandinavians a long time.

Learn when to pull out all the stops and above all learn never to give up. The last few years have seen heroic drives by people like Markku Alen and Russell Brookes from nearly last place (after an excursion) up into the top six.

Never give up unless of course you have a terminal accident. And you need to recognise that if you are trying hard and hoping to go places, then sooner or later you are going to have an accident. Rallying is a relatively safe sport but there are no special techniques for having happy accidents, although it does seem as if some drivers bear charmed lives—or have such developed reflexes that they can stay in touch with things later than lesser mortals.

Don't misunderstand us—we are *not* advocating an irresponsible approach which puts you in a ditch on every rally. What we are saying is that if you are to find your limit then sooner or later you are likely to over-cook things and come unstuck. How you learn from the experience and how you progress as a result will dictate just how good a driver you become.

One final footnote on rally driving: **never** try to improve your performance by taking drugs. They are unlikely to make you quicker, they could mar your judgement and cause an accident. And most important of all, rallying just doesn't need the drug taking scandals which beset other sports.

8 Rally navigation

Having devoted a chapter to developing the *prima ballerinas* it is now time to introduce the *corps de ballet*, that brave body always destined to play the role of bridesmaids, the poor little Cinderellas hidden away from the limelight—the navigators or co-drivers!

The navigator/co-driver enjoys little of the glamour but most of the worries, (ever counted the number of co-drivers with grey hair/no hair/ulcers?). At the professional level the co-driver only earns a fraction of the top drivers' fees yet frequently finds himself the subject of abuse and criticism and ends up with all the dirty jobs.

In the event of a breakdown it will be the co-driver who walks for miles over frozen moorland to summon help whilst the driver sleeps in a cosy rug. Before the rally it will be the co-driver who sits in his hotel room checking his pace-notes and studying the regulations whilst the driver goes to a glittering pre-rally reception to meet Miss World. After being thrown about and pummelled on the rally it will be the co-driver who misses the post-rally dinner because he is checking the results. Blessed are the meek.

The sole redeeming feature of navigating is that it is the cheapest way into the sport, and if you're lucky enough to reach the very top and sit alongside the world's great drivers as part of a Works Team you'll appreciate the privileged position you occupy; all the horrors and hardships will have been worth it.

However, before we discuss the craft at which you'll need to become perfect, let us briefly discuss the terminology used in describing the poor creature, for he doesn't even possess a proper title!

Basically, the navigator tends to be so-called when he's conducting the map work on a road event and where he will never be expected to touch the steering wheel. Co-drivers were originally called such on the bigger Internationals where navigation was not too difficult and where they might be required to drive, albeit on easier sections.

Now the term co-driver is used for the passenger on even the smallest stage event when there is absolutely no likelihood of him taking the wheel. On anything but a navigational road rally we should really describe him as the Office Manager for that is what he is—a highly organised office manager who can drive safely (if he has to give his precious partner a rest) and who probably has a good knowledge of psychology, mathematics, languages, geography and economics. If you qualify on all counts, telephone your nearest team manager immediately. If you fail to qualify, don't worry, we've yet to find anyone who does.

A good navigator (and we'll call him that for the rest of this chapter) will start by gaining as much experience as possible in every type of event from the smallest treasure hunt upwards. He will be a keen motor club member—probably be involved in running events and committee work as all this develops the ability to organise, which is the navigator's job. By helping organise rallies one begins to understand the workings of organisers' minds and this can be very useful for a competitor.

The navigator will be a tidy-minded individual and will keep everything in its place in the car, and although he will let the driver look after the mechanical bits he will know where the jack, the spare fuses and the tow-rope are stowed.

Now on to the navigators' equipment.

The most important, and probably the first item to be purchased by a navigator will be a map. Assuming you are starting in British rallies this will inevitably come from the glorious range of Ordnance Survey Maps, most likely one of the 1.50,000 series; these give a scale of approximately $1\frac{1}{4}$ inches to the mile and are now used by all British rally organisers. The organisers of any rally will specify the maps to be used on the event, and you should obtain these maps in good time and prepare them for the rally.

Ordnance Survey Maps are available in folded or unfolded form, and it is a matter of personal preference which you use. Most people take folded versions as they are easier to store and file.

When you buy your Ordnance Survey Map you will notice that it is covered by thin lines forming small squares—these lines are part of the National Grid which covers the country and is based on a point in the English Channel, south-west of Lands End. The figures by the lines along the edges of the map represent their distances in kilometers, east and north of this origin. If total measurements from the point off Lands End were taken, the number of kilometers would be too large for practical use, so the figures are repeated every 100 kilometers and each 100 kilometer square is designated by two letters. The small diagram on the bottom of each map shows the incidence of grid letters on it. You will rarely, if ever, encounter the letters on a rally, the actual map being indicated by its number and you'll become very familiar with these map numbers and know that sheet 136 is "Newtown and Llanidloes", sheet 95 is the Isle of Man and so on.

The driver can help his navigator by reading out route instructions and map references.

When plotting a map reference always plot 'eastings' first; these are the numbers printed along the top and bottom edges of the map. Next plot the 'northings'—the numbers printed down both sides. There are several catch phrases to help you to remember which to plot first, one of the more printable being: "along the passage and up the stairs". In other words, first look *along* the bottom edge, then *up* the sides. To make it easier to plot a reference, every tenth grid line is printed slightly heavier than the rest. In a six figure reference the first three figures represent tens, units and tenths of kilometers east and the last three represent those to to the north (see diagram). With practice you should become adept at plotting references and the more expert navigators can manage at least two or three a minute when stationary and can also keep up a healthy batting average when the car is moving.

Practise plotting as much as you can and you'll soon speed up—but always take extra care with references like 010101 or 696969. In order to give a really accurate plot (possibly a road beside a grass

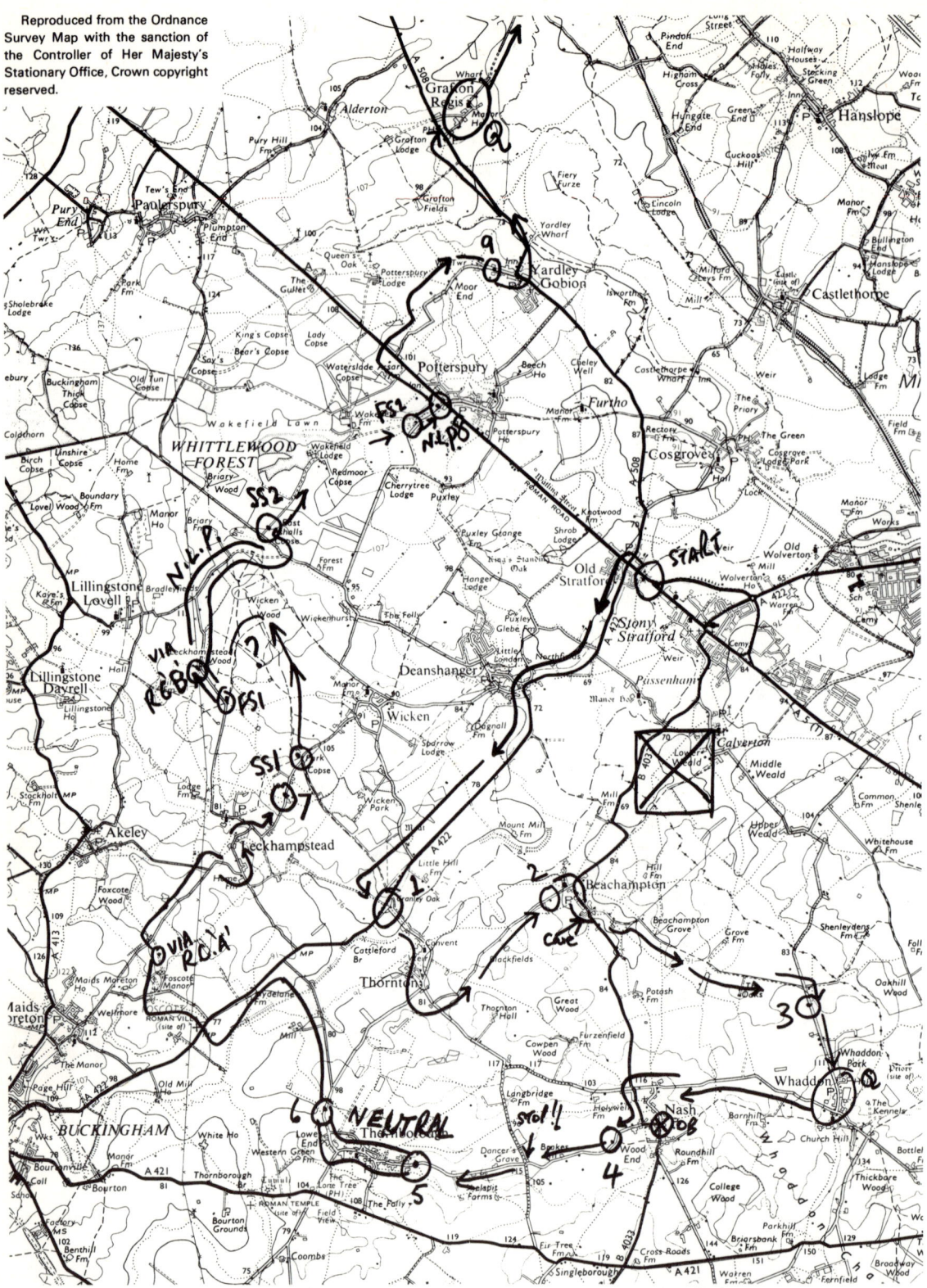

The route should be marked on a map as clearly as possible, in pencil. Arrows and lines must not obscure any bends or road to be used. Note how clearly the "Out of Bounds" areas are marked, together with "Quiet Zones", "Neutral" and "No Lateness Penalty" sections — forgetting these can lead to heavy penalties. Note that extra comments have been taken from the road book and added to the maps such as "Care" after TC2 and, "Stop" at X-roads after TC4. Special Stage Starts and Finishes are marked clearly.

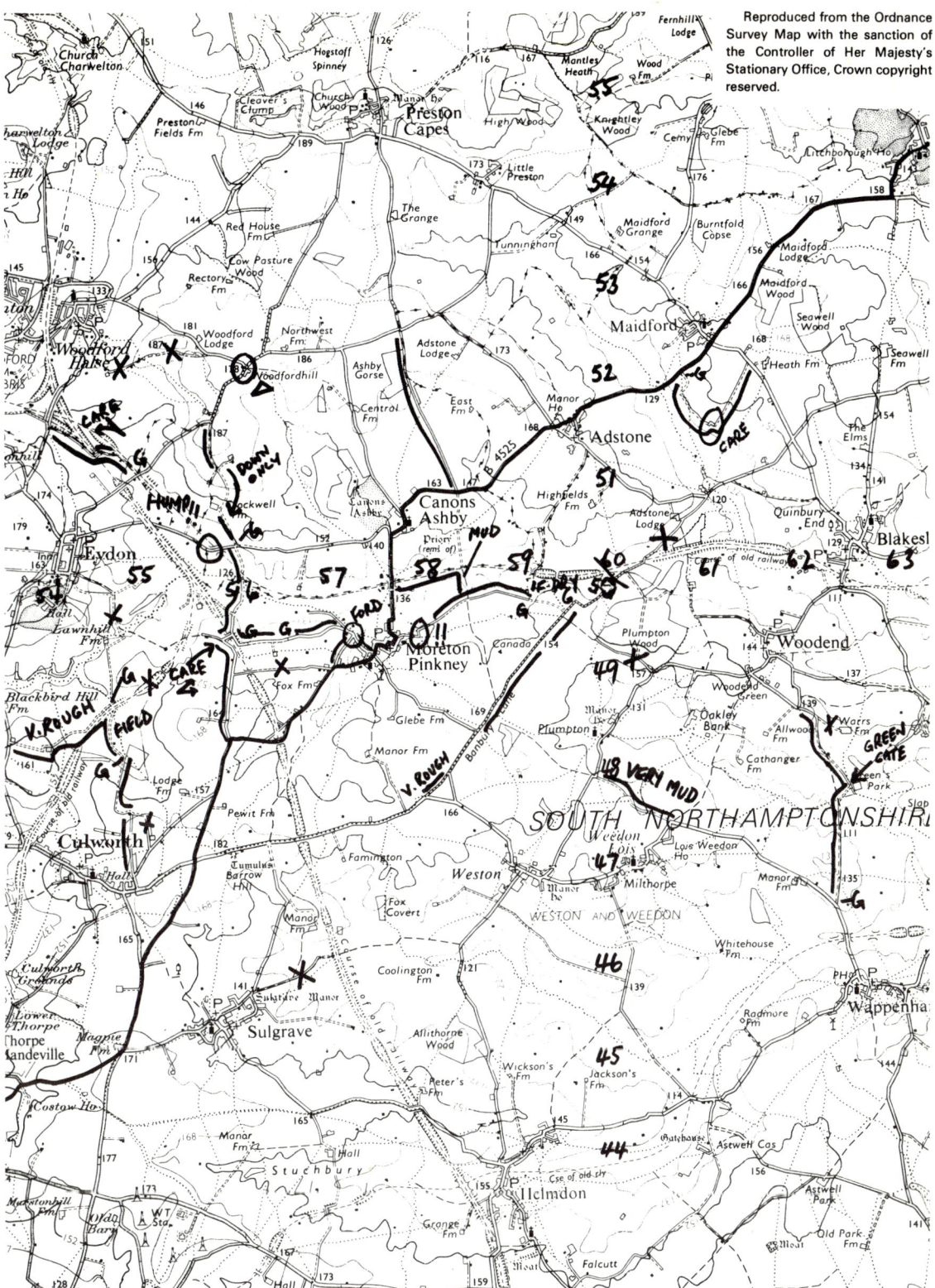

Most navigators add markings to their maps, such as the eastings and northings as on this 1:50,000 O.S. map, to save having to refer to the edges when plotting references. A 'goer' or 'non-goer' in the case of a white road is marked by a simple line alongside or an "X" across the road (taking care not to obscure any important printing). Special features marked are gate at 560504, bad hump at 558503, grass triangle at 562522 and dangerous corner at 579494. Budding navigators should note that this example of map marking on sheet 152 is purely for demonstration purposes.

An illuminated map magnifier is necessary for road rally navigators. This one is made in strong PVC and carries a power- ful lens and bulb. For British use a romer baseplate is incorporated.

triangle—beloved by rally organisers) you may be given an eight figure reference, but it is more common for organisers to stick to 'halves' and so a reference will be shown as $100\frac{1}{2}200\frac{1}{2}$ (or, as some purists may prefer, 10052005).

In order to plot references quickly and accurately it is necessary to use a "romer". This is a small plastic device, of which there are several makes and is the navigator's prime tool of his trade. A romer has the scale of the map broken down into tenths and by sliding this along the maps having found the appropriate kilometer square, you can measure off the exact reference accurately and quickly. Romers carry scales of several maps—possibly 1–50,000, 1–63,360 (the old 1 inch to the mile maps, now replaced in Britain by the 1.50,000 scale) and even 1.126720 scale; this $\frac{1}{2}$ inch to the mile scale is used mostly in Ireland.

If you are planning to use the romer only with 1.50,000 maps you might round off the other three corners so that you can find the necessary scale instantly; this can save time. The romer should be placed on a loop of string, worn round the neck—there's nothing so elusive as a 'stringless' romer in a bouncing rally car.

Ordnance Survey maps are easily obtainable and there is an official stockist in practically every town. It is advisable to purchase your maps from one stockist so that you build up a relationship with the retailer; they may then be more helpful when you require maps which are out of stock.

Although British Ordnance Survey maps are the clearest and carry most detail and are possibly the best maps in the world, they do require additional information to be added for rally use. Extra markings (shown in the illustration) should be added in waterproof ink—care must be taken to avoid obliterating information already on the map. A simple blue ball-point is as good as anything and marking should be kept as simple as possible.

To save having to refer to the edges when plotting references, extra 'eastings' and 'northings' should be added to the map, ideally on every 10 kilometer grid line.

A road which is shown in white on the map may be passable or it may be unsurfaced and peter out into a bog or chassis-breaking impasse. In rally parlance these roads are 'goers' or 'non-goers' and as time progresses the rally navigator will gain more information about these; this information should be added to the map. We recommended a simple line alongside the road or an 'X' to indicate goers and non-goers respectively.

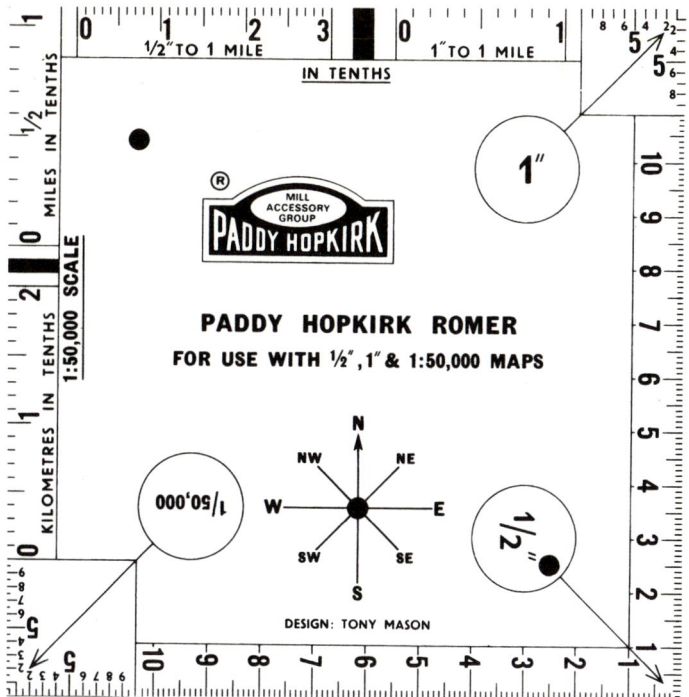

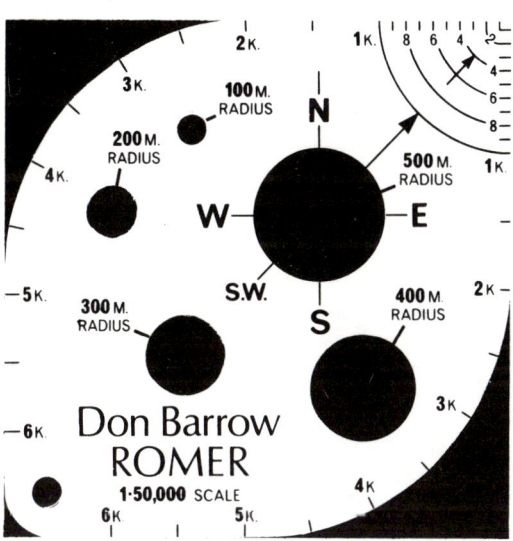

The romer is the navigator's most important tool of his trade. There are several types. The Don Barrow model carries holes of different diameter for marking noise areas. The Paddy Hopkirk model can be used with three map scales.

Hump-backed bridges, difficult junctions, grass triangles, fords, bad bends, known mud patches, etc., can all be added and built up from information gathered through experience (often bitter) or from reading rally reports in newspapers and magazines.

When you learn something new on a rally, mark it on the map you are using in pencil, then later mark it permanently. Speaking of white roads, you should remember that a broken line along a road does not refer to the standard of road but tells you that the road has no fence or wall.

Mark the number of adjoining maps on each map edge and if you know any particularly tricky section where junctions and tracks hover between the edges of maps, 'doctor' the maps by drawing on the details. Maps can quickly wear at the folds, so a piece of Sellotape stuck on the backs of the corner folds can help to preserve the maps and avoid your trying to navigate your driver through holes.

Make sure you know how to read a map and if you are about to venture onto new territory, have a good look at the map to familiarise yourself with the layout of the land. You should know all the symbols used on the maps; if not, study the key printed at the bottom.

Pay attention to the classification of roads and also the various lines used for electricity grids, pipelines and boundaries; these can be mixed up easily. Churches, Youth Hostels, telephone kiosks, milestones and bridges are all good landmarks and help to keep you on route during a rally. When studying new country, pay close attention to contour lines to get some idea of how hilly the country is: the height of contours are written in the contour lines at intervals along their length. On Ordnance Survey maps they are printed so that they read facing uphill which provides a quick check as to the direction of the slope. Contours close together mean steep slopes and contours further apart mean more gentle ones.

To put the route of a rally on the map you should use a soft pencil (2B or 3B); never have a very sharp point as this may be difficult to erase. Always carry a lot of pencils—they keep breaking and have a habit of jumping out of your fingers and sliding under the seat at the most crucial moments.

Keep markings simple and never rub fingers over the map as the pencil lead quickly becomes ingrained and makes the map less clear for future occasions.

It is usually best to draw a circle for a control and indicate your route by a line alongside the road with the odd arrow to remind you of your direction of travel.

Noise zones, no-lateness junctions, neutral sections (where you must *not* make up time) must all be marked clearly. Mark where you change from one map to the other by writing in the margin "CM to ..." with the number of the map you are moving onto.

Although you'll have time cards, roadbooks, regulations and so on in the car, the map is your *working document* and as much information as possible must be kept on it.

Always use a cardboard map board—never, never use metal, wood or anything hard; an accident can have very painful consequences if an unyielding board is rammed into your pelvis. The cardboard should be approximately 18 inches square and is purely used to hold all the maps in position. Some people clip them in position—others let them lie loose. A map board with rally information marked on it is helpful—information

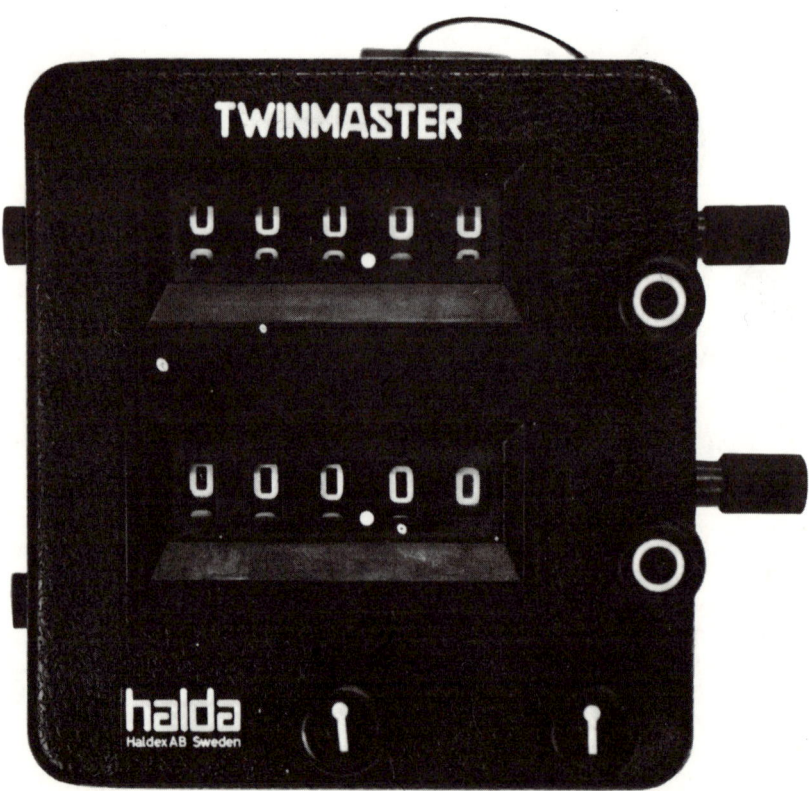

The Halda Twinmaster has two dials so that, for instance, a special stage can be logged on one while the total rally distance continues on the other.

The Terra Trip relies on modern electronics although the pair of clocks to the left are still 'wind-up'. Before long, quartz clocks must surely take over.

like average speeds, maximum and minimum times allowed etc. (one will be penalised for completing sections in less than three-quarters of the official time. The equations for working out average speeds, lengths of section etc are also useful.

A simple clipboard should be used as well with important rally documents like route and time cards etc., fixed to it. It is better to have time cards tightly clipped in position—marshals prefer something hard to rest on when signing your card. Incidentally it is advisable to work out a routine for marshals; you may prefer to open the door and let them lean in. You can shine the light on the board for them and all of this saves time for you.

On many rallies you will be given small route check cards and these should be kept in a pouch or special secure envelope as it can be heartbreaking to discover the loss of a card when you have completed a two-hundred mile rally.

A map measurer (called an opisometer, consisting of a small wheel and dial) is useful to carry, as is a Blackwell Calculator (a sort of circular slide rule). A pocket calculator (for calculating times and average speeds) should be carried, ideally one with a built-in stop watch. Navigators should keep a close watch on silicone chip technology (not Harry Ramsden's—electronics) because the dramatic advances in the last couple of years seem likely to continue and could all make things easier for navigators.

These items should all be stored carefully and always in the same place, say in a door pocket or a document case under the dashboard.

Maps, other than the ones you are using, should be kept in sequence and in a handy position. Another useful tip is to take a few maps of surrounding areas as you never know when you may have to go off route in the event of a diversion or retirement (or quite simply through getting lost!).

Some method of magnifying the map is essential. There are illuminated magnifiers which work from

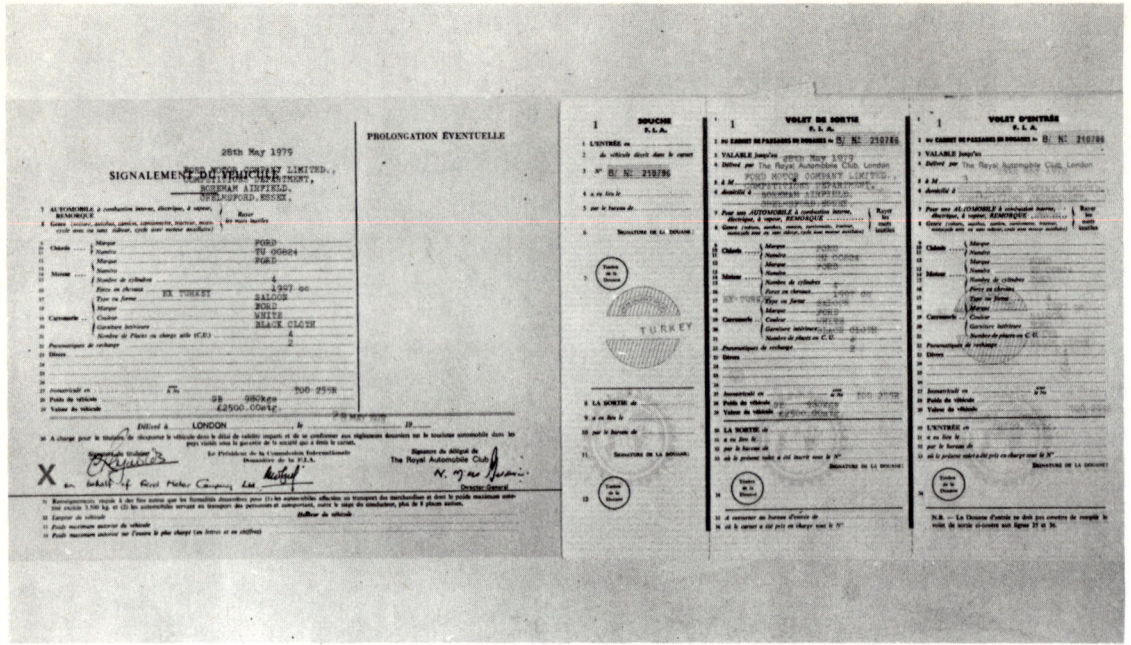

The co-driver's role as 'office manager' may include responsibility for the "Carnet de Passage en Douanes" — in other words, the document which helps you get spares through Customs. Almost as complicated as an homologation form

batteries and whilst these are useful as spares they are not recommended for fulltime use as the batteries might run down at a crucial moment. (In any case, it is better to use the driver's power thus saving navigator's expenses on torch batteries!).

There *are* navigators still using the old Eolites once used by R.A.F. navigators in World War II but now the most popular is the Don Barrow Light which has a built-in scale base (removable) and powerful magnifying lens. Many top road rally crews even carry a spare.

If you wear spectacles (many navigators do) remember to keep them in position with a cord at the back of the neck. Always carry a spare pair.

Your driver will probably expect you to be the bookworm! You should be the one to send for regulations and you should then study them very carefully. If you are interested in an event then submit your entry early because the better rallies are often over-subscribed.

You must know what time you need to report for scrutineering, when and how the route will be given out, how much time you can make up, the difference between stage penalties and road marks, the penalties for lateness, etc. Many of these are very small points, but a mistake with any one of them could wreck your chances on an event.

When you get to the start of a rally the route you are given is obviously of vital importance, and so is any list of black-spots and prohibited areas which you *must* observe. Drivers are notorious for wandering off aimlessly during the preliminaries to the start of a rally, so find your man a particular job to keep him busy.

On the majority of rallies you will find yourself plotting the route from map references, often with directions of approach and departure stipulated. Sometimes, particularly on smaller events, you may be given the route in more bizarre ways but if the rally is properly run this needn't throw you because no responsible organiser will risk the public nuisance of cars milling about lost because he was too smart in his route instructions.

Most crews incur 'fails' at some time in their career because of wrong directions of approach or departure. Always check these very thoroughly when they are stipulated and remember not to get west and east confused. You might think this is elementary but a great number of experienced competitors very easily confuse south-west with south-east and, needless to say, it is a favourite trick of organisers to place controls at junctions requiring an approach from one of these two directions.

Once you are under way on the event, keep your driver in touch with what is happening, but don't babble on too much; give him a chance to settle down, perhaps calling out the occasional phone box or something clearly visible to help him build his confidence in you. When you are starting as a navigator, don't try to read every bend on the map to the driver because you will probably find that although you are making a very good job of it, you are actually on the wrong road!

MAP	INTER MILES	TOTAL MILES	LOCATION		ROAD NO.	DIRECTION

MOFFAT   TO   CARDRONA   30.50 MILES   1 HRS.   01 MINS.

MAP	INTER MILES	TOTAL MILES	LOCATION		ROAD NO.	DIRECTION
78	0.00	0.00	TIME CONTROL TC53B			
	0.07	0.07				
	0.02	0.09		 (A708)		
VIA 79 73	21.36	21.45	GORDON ARMS HOTEL		B709	PEEBLES
	6.68	28.13				
	0.43	28.56	TRAQUAIR		B7062	PEEBLES
	1.84	30.40				ENTER FOREST
	0.10	30.50				

TIME CONTROL ATC54 – CARDRONA

SPECIAL STAGE SS54 – CARDRONA

A page from the roadbook of the R.A.C. Rally. Both intermediate and cumulative mileage distances are shown. Note the helpful map numbers in the left-hand column. The 'Tulip arrow' method of route instruction is in world-wide use.

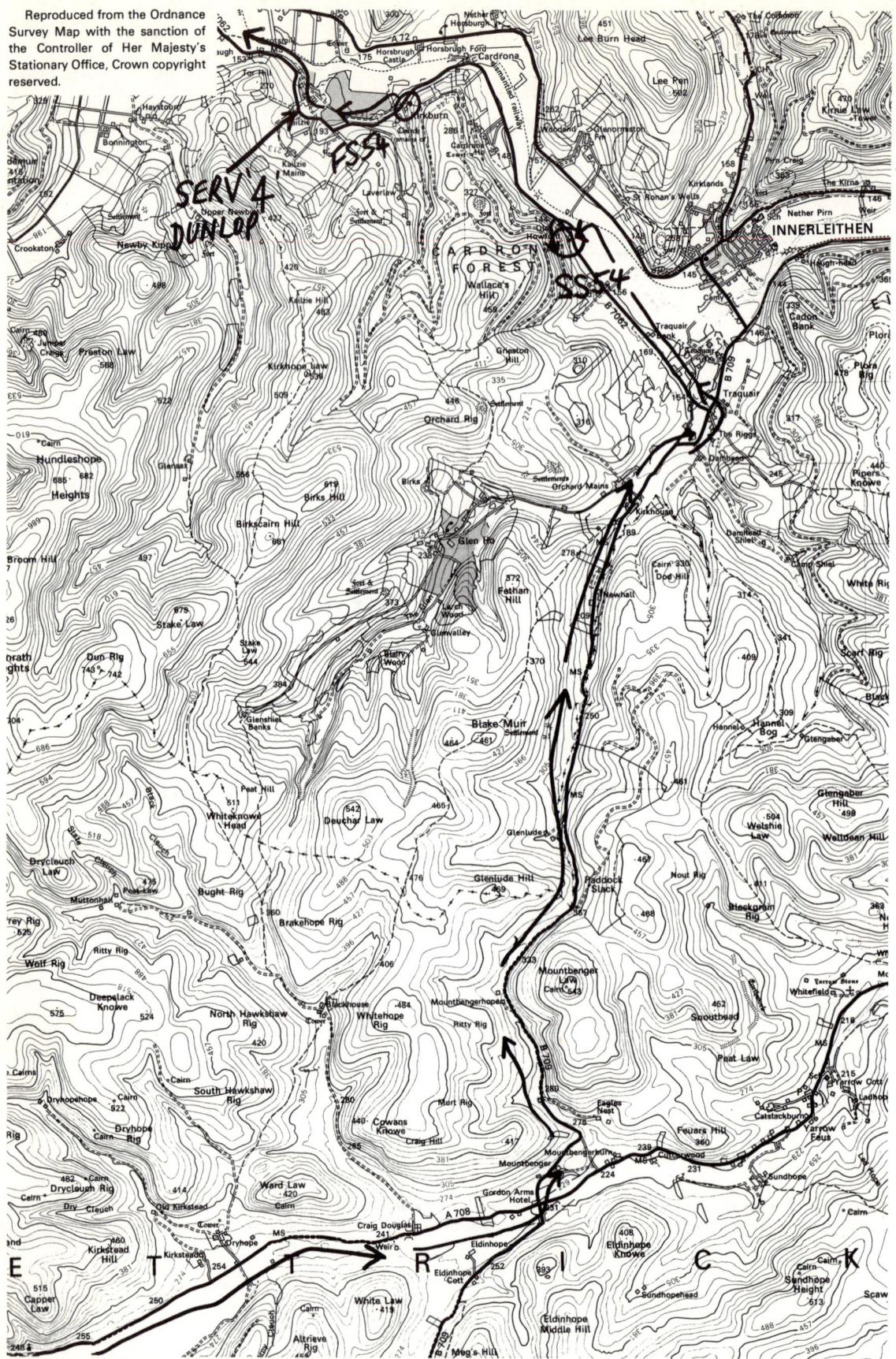

The page of the R.A.C. roadbook featured on page 67 would be transferred to the map like this. The number of a service crew and its location have also been marked by the co-driver.

Above all, *concentrate* (that word again!) on making sure that you are on the right road at all times, and that you guide your driver down the correct slots (turnings) without overshooting. When you can do this consistently well, start to call out the bad bends, then with experience you can start to call out more gradual ones; how far you pursue this depends on just what information your driver needs. If he is inexperienced he'll probably be frightening himself so much that he won't be paying all that much attention to what you are saying anyway. Concentrate all the time; this will keep you on the ball and will also reassure the driver.

Marshals are an important part of a rally; always be nice to them. Present your route card to them properly and if you haven't got a light on the roof to help them, hold your map light over your route card. Unless you have a lot of time in hand, don't get too involved in chatting to marshals as you may break your concentration. Try not to shout or argue with marshals as you are seldom likely to win; they have the upper hand! Some people still try to 'shout up' the time or bully marshals into giving them the time they want but most marshals have already been warned of this trick.

Make sure a marshal signs in the right place and *check* his work immediately. His is an arduous job and inevitably human error creeps in—particularly on a long, cold, wet night. Keep your road book clean if you can and if a marshal happens to make a mistake in entering a time or direction of approach then get him to alter it and sign the correction immediately—it will be difficult to get things changed later.

If you can, stay in the car at controls. Check your map work and time cards. Don't be eager to leave the car and blab your times to other competitors; they may be encouraged to try harder and pull back a deficit!

After a stop of any kind, remember to tell your driver what the next section is like—it is *your* fault if he sets off at half throttle when he ought to be pressing on.

We've talked about the importance of timekeeping—let's now mention the types of timing.

On most road rallies the marshals will hold the watches—usually clear, accurate, waterproof clocks or digital timepieces. Marshals will read off the time in hours and minutes, always reading to the previous minute e.g., 06 hour 37 mins. 59 secs. will read as 06.37. On some 'selective' sections or on special tie-deciding parts seconds may be used.

A marshal's timepiece will either be set to the time of day, or more likely, to "Targa Time". This takes its name from the rally that first adopted this timing—Oxford University's Targa Rusticana, one of the classic road rallies of the sixties. It's a very clever but simple idea. The clock at the start of the rally is set so that car number 1 will depart at 00.01, car number 2 at 00.02 and so on. Car number 61 will depart at 01.01. The timepiece at each subsequent control is set back by the amount of time allocated to the section. Therefore, if car number 1 is on time at every control he'll clock in at 00.01 everywhere. It's easy for marshals to operate (less likelihood of a mistake) and easy for results teams.

Organisers will set and seal all timepieces prior to the rally. These will be hired from companies who specialise in hiring out timekeeping equipment to motor clubs.

At one time competitors carried the watches used to record their progress but today only the smallest club rally provides competitors with 'sealed watches'. These are set back from BBC time by their competition number so making them all due at each control at the time shown on the routecard. This system of timekeeping is open to abuse by competitors and marshals so is now never used on better events.

Stage rallies are usually timed at normal time of day and the stages themselves are always timed to the second or even fraction of a second. Generally speaking, the bigger the rally the better the timepieces but all should be set by competent registered timekeepers. Printing clocks are also used occasionally.

At the end of a special stage a marshall will signal or phone through the precise moment that each car crosses the flying finish line to another marshal holding the watch further along the stage; cars stop at this marshal to have times recorded.

When you move on to international events, the navigator becomes very much an office manager. You will need maps of course—quarter inch maps in the UK are close to the Michelins you will use on the Continent and will give you a feel for the scale— but there will be a lot more than maps to think about!

You will have to arrange insurance, hotels, passports, visas (if any), boat tickets, Carnets, maybe airline tickets, etc, etc, etc! And by the way you will need a "Foreign Event Visa" from the R.A.C. which allows you to take part in overseas events— this only costs a few pounds and includes the basic medical insurance.

Then you may have to organise fuel arrangements, service points—where and when brake pads should be renewed and so on. You will probably be in charge of planning service.

Realise that overseas events are not run on the same lines as British events—so don't assume domestic custom and practice necessarily applies—and it is important that you study the regulations carefully and make sure that you know what you can and cannot do without penalty. Ask the organisers and the more experienced competitors if you have any doubts whatsoever.

Be particularly careful about booking in at controls as many people have incurred 'early penalty' marks because they didn't study the regulations properly.

Don't forget to make sure you have all the necessary inoculations for the countries you are visiting

SS13: MOSCHOKARIA.

II

10.0 KMS.   SMOOTH, TWISTY DIRT.

NOTES START FROM JUNCTION: ↰ (100m. AFTER WATER TROUGH.)

Č   ER   <u>L</u>   <u>R</u>

EL   C_{KEEP R}   ER   100

E̊R   SO   Č   EL-ER

ER—   <u>CARE</u>   C-KL

♭ER-EL

KR   KL   <u>HPR</u>—<u>HPL</u>

<u>CARE</u> ♭KR>—<u>BL</u>   L̈   R̈

KL (HOUSE) — KR/BRIDGE

II

FLAT CREST,   EASY RIGHT,   <u>LEFT</u>,   <u>RIGHT</u>,

EASY LEFT,   CREST, KEEP RIGHT   EASY RIGHT, ONE INWARD

·FLAT RIGHT,   FIFTY,   FLAT CREST,   EASY LEFT INTO EASY RIGHT

EASY RIGHT INTO <u>CARE</u> CREST INTO K LEFT

LONG EASY RIGHT INTO EASY LEFT

K RIGHT,   K LEFT,   <u>HAIRPIN RIGHT</u> INTO <u>HAIRPIN LEFT</u>

<u>CARE</u> LONG K RIGHT TIGHTENS INTO <u>BAD LEFT</u>   ABSOLUTE LEFT, ABSOLUTE RIGHT

K LEFT (—) INTO K RIGHT OVER BRIDGE "

└→ 'HOUSE' IS NOT CALLED, FOR CO-DRIVER'S GUIDANCE ONLY, OR TO HELP IF LOST!

'Pace Notes' are essential for a good performance on a non-secret route. These 'Moschokaria' notes were prepared by Jim Porter for an Acropolis Rally. Below the notes is shown how they would be read to a driver. When writing notes always vary the length of lines — this breaks up the page and prevents the wrong line being read — and try to avoid starting successive lines with the same symbol or word. Number every page at the top AND bottom.

(making sure you have them in good time and have left the required space of time between injections). Don't become a sort of travelling Boots, but do take the odd tablet for stomach upsets, diarrhoea, headaches and sunstroke: your doctor will advise you.

On most stage events and nearly all Internationals you will encounter 'Tulip arrows' because they are by far the simplest way of indicating a route. Tulip arrows are so-called because they were first used on the Dutch Tulip Rally many years ago—not because some of the diagrams look like tulips. Unless you have absolute faith in the organisers, plot a Tulip route on the maps then put the map numbers in the road book (the R.A.C. Rally does this for you), then even if you just use the road book you will be able to dig out the appropriate map if you hit problems.

If you make route or navigational notes Tulip arrows are by far the best way because you can easily and diagrammatically portray each junction. If you are contemplating doing a winter event, remember that snow might cover milestones and road markings, so only record items which will stand proud.

Pace notes play a prominent part in many International events and although you'll be well advised to steer clear of them in the earlier stages of your career you'll find them a necessary part of your life later on. Making pace notes and all forms of recceing is regarded by many as boring, futile and a complete waste of time. It's certainly very time and petrol-consuming but if other crews are using notes, you'll have to do likewise to stay competitive.

Pace notes are a way by which the co-driver can remind or tell the driver about the road they are approaching. Ideally the notes should be made by the crews themselves although it may be necessary to use notes made by other members of a team on occasions. This can be dangerous and there have been expensive accidents as a result of the misinterpretation of instructions perhaps because the terminology used by one crew differed from that used by another.

If pace notes have been made properly (preferably by several runs over a stage) they can be both fast and safe. Pace notes can be a great help to performance on a stage because they present a picture to the

Pace notes for long distance events take the form of route instructions and carry many descriptive passages. Note 'tourist guide' references to animals and rivers on this page of Safari notes. The panel of times is redrawn from the official roadbook and the co-driver's own comments about lateness added.

The Cowan/Malkin/Broad Mercedes-Benz used these notes to win the last London-Sydney Rally. They were hurriedly made by the crew a short time before the Australian section began. The notes show a desert section which, with its numerous closed gates, presented something of a navigational nightmare. The "V" symbol refers to a dip and the rather long abbreviations give information about gates, etc – "C.O.R.O.A." means catch-on-right-opens-away, which meant that whoever opened the gate knew exactly which side to run.

26. If the entrant is not a crew member the first driver nominated on the entry form shall be deemed to be his agent. Wherever an entrant is referred to in these regulations this shall also mean his agent, if appropriate.

C—Eligible Cars

27. All cars must comply with Appendix 'J' to the International sporting Code and must be individually licensed for the road, i.e. competing cars cannot be driven on any form of Trade plate. An F.I.A. Form of Recognition for each competing car SHALL be produced by the entrant at scrutineering and on official demand at any other time during the event. In determining a car's appropriate class the engine capacity will be deemed to be that on the Form of Recognition.

28. An entrant is deemed to have full knowledge of his/her car and to vouch for its eligibility by the act of presenting the car for scrutiny at the start.

29. The entry will be divided into eight classes:

Class (1)	Group 1	Up to 1300 cc.
Class (2)	Group 1	Over 1300 up to 1600 cc.
Class (3)	Group 1	Over 1600 cc.
Class (4)	Group 2	Up to 1600 cc.
Class (5)	Group 2	Over 1600 cc.
Class (6)	Groups 3 & 4	Up to 1600 cc.
Class (7)	Groups 3 & 4	Over 1600 up to 2000 cc.
Class (8)	Groups 3 & 4	Over 2000 cc.

30. Each class, or series of classes as amalgamated in accordance with Article 40(g), shall include at the start at least five cars of the cylinder-capacity concerned. Should a class or amalgamated classes not include enough cars prior to the start, the organisers may make further amalgamation up to the start in order to provide for a minimum of five starters.

31. The use of non-skid attachments (which includes tyres with studs or spikes of metal or other material) other than "chains" is prohibited during the event, unless the organisers announce otherwise. Furthermore, any "chains" not of a type normally on retail sale must be submitted for the approval of the Promoters. Tyres with any form of metal in the tread compound are not permitted.

32. The addition of sump or chassis guards is permitted.

33. *All* cars must at all times during the competition:
    (a) Carry fire extinguishers of at least 5kg. total capacity, contained in not more than two separate units.
    (b) Be fitted with a windscreen of Laminated glass.
    (c) Be fitted with a safety roll-bar or cage complying with F.I.A. regulations.
    (d) Carry a reflective red triangle for use by the crew.

9. The repairing of cars during rest periods is forbidden. See paragraph 18. If during the Rally a car is found not to comply with the traffic safety regulations, the Chief Scrutineer may order repairs to be made even during 'parc fermé'. Only the repairs ordered by the Chief Scrutineer can be made and under the control of the organizers.

10. Servicing is not allowed on the traffic lanes on any main road. Competitor discovered by Stewards, Organizers or police doing service on these roads may be excluded from the event.

11. All competitors must use the official number plates and side numbers which bear the advertisement of Oy Konela Ab.

12. The Organizers will reserve place for advertisements of 600 cm² each, which will be affixed on bonnet, boot lid, front doors, front wings and on the roof behind the windshield of the rally cars. If a competitor refuses to accept such Organizers' advertisements as do not contradict with his own, he must pay a 50 % higher entry fee. These advertisements must not be removed during the Rally.

13. Competitors can have their own advertisements on the cars, except on windshield, windows, bonnet and front doors. Advertising of alcoholic drinks is forbidden according to the Finnish law.

14. In the case of an accident competitors must give immediate assistance. The loss of time thus incurred, provided that it does not exceed half an hour, may be deducted from the competitor's driving time on presentation of a written application.

15. START

1. The start of the Rally will take place in Jyväskylä on August 26, 1977, at 18 01 hours at one minute intervals.
2. The competitors must check in at Controls in the order given in the Time Cards.
3. The official Rally time is the same as the time signal of the Finnish Broadcasting Company.
4. If a competitor drops out of the Rally he must inform the Rally Headquarters without fail and he must immediately remove his Rally numbers and the advertisements affixed by the organizers.

16. CONTROLS

1. All controls will be marked by means of standardised panels complying with the drawings below.

No. 1   No. 2   No. 3   No. 4

Most International organisers provide English translations for their regulations. These are pages from Finland's 1000 Lakes Rally. Note the self-explanatory international symbols for controls etc.

ITINÉRAIRE: LONDRES

Contrôles horaires et de passage	Distances partielles	Distances totales	Temps idéaux
LONDRES .... Douvres (C.P.)		0	
CALAIS..................... Rouen (C.P.)	119	119	6 h 00
ALENÇON	368	487	7 h 23
BOURGES	275	762	5 h 30
TROYES	226	988	4 h 32
REIMS .... Saint-Die (C.P.) Morteau (C.P.)	127	1115	2 h 33
SAINT-CLAUDE	590	1705	11 h 49
LA MURE.....................	213	1918	4 h 14
GAP	65	1983	2 h 20
MONACO.....................	513	2496	9 h 02

Cartes Michelin utilisées pour le parcours en France:
Nº 51 - 52 - 60 - 64 - 68 - 69 - 65 - 61 - 56 - 57 - 55 - 61 - 62 - 66 - 70 - 74 - 77 - 81 - 84 - 195.

Monte Carlo Rally organisers give route details in their regulations. This page shows the route for London starters ...

Communes	Routes	Distances part.	Distances tot.	Horaire approximatif
Nuit du Jeudi 26 au Vendredi 27 Janvier 1978.				
9e Étape: ST.-SAUVEUR S/TINÉE - ROQUESTERON: 78 km - Temps idéal: 1 h 34.				
7e Épreuve Spéciale Chronométrée 22 km env. — **ST.-SAUVEUR S/TINEE**	D 30			de 3 h 39 à 5 h 19
ROUBION				
COL DE LA COUILLOLE				
BEUIL	D 30	22	22	de 4 h 03 à 5 h 59
Bif. D 30 / D 28..	D 28	1	23	
Pont de Cians	N 202	22	45	de 4 h 28 à 6 h 08
Puget Theniers ...	D 2211A	7	52	de 4 h 36 à 6 h 16
Col St.-Raphael ...		8	60	de 4 h 45 à 6 h 25
Bif. 2211A / D 427	D 2211A			
Bif. 2211A / D 10..				
Bif. 2211A / D 17..	D 17	7	67	de 4 h 55 à 6 h 35
Sigale		3	70	
ROQUESTERON		8	26	de 5 h 13 à 6 h 53
10e Étape: ROQUESTERON - BIF. D 53 / D 22: 91 km - Temps idéal: 1 h 49				
8e Épreuve Spéciale Chronométrée 19 km env. — **ROQUESTERON**	D 1			de 5 h 14 à 6 h 54
CONSEGUDES				
LES FERRES				
BOUYON	D 1	19	19	de 5 h 34 à 7 h 14
Le Broc		8	27	de 5 h 44 à 7 h 24
C.P. — Bif. D 1 / D 2209	D 2209	4	31	de 5 h 49 à 7 h 29
Bif. D 2209 / D 17 ..	D 17			
Bif. D 17 / N 202..	N 202	11	42	de 6 h 01 à 7 h 41
St.-Martin du Var ..	D 20	2	44	
La Roquette s/Var ...				
Levens	D 19	10	54	de 6 h 14 à 7 h 54
Bif. D 19 / D 815 ..	D 815	7,5	61,5	
C.P. — Châteauneuf de Contes		11,5	73	de 6 h 34 à 8 h 14
Bif. D 815 / D 15 ..	D 15			
Bif. D 15 / D 2204 ..	D 2204	5	78	de 6 h 42 à 8 h 22
Bif. D 2204 / D 21 ..	D 21	1	79	de 6 h 50 à 8 h 30
La Grave		6	85	
Bif. D 21 / D 53..	D 53			
BIF. D 53 / D 22		6	91	de 7 h 03 à 8 h 43
11e Étape: BIF. D 53 / D 22 - MONACO: 27 km - Temps idéal: 0 h 40.				
9e Épreuve Spéc. Chrono. 8,5 km env. — { **BIF. D 53 / D 22**	D 22			de 7 h 04 à 8 h 44
COL DE LA MADONE..				
STE-AGNES		8,5	8,5	de 7 h 14 à 8 h 54
C.P. — Bif. D 22 / D 23	D 23	7	15,5	
Menton	N7	4	19,5	de 7 h 26 à 9 h 06
Bif. N 7 / N 559.....	N 559	3	22,5	de 7 h 30 à 9 h 10
Bif. N 559 / N 564 A....	N 559			
MONACO		4,5	27	de 7 h 44 à 9 h 24

... and this the more detailed instructions for the final night of the event.

driver of the road which he cannot fully see; they help the driver to keep up the speed of the car and he should be able to position the car properly at all times.

If possible, pace notes should be finally checked at rally speeds, preferably in a rally car (initial note-making can be done in a much slower vehicle, say a hire car).

When making notes it is best to write them in rough form, then copy them into a neater style after checking. Pocket tape recorders are not really a good idea—you may put in too much detail and if they decide not to operate at a crucial moment you will have nothing to copy out. Put in various geographic notes (but not too many) as you will be able to keep your place better. Mention the odd signpost, house or sign, and keep your notes in a spiral bound book, written in black so that they can be photocopied and pages interchanged if necessary.

The language used in pace notes must be clear and fully understood between driver and navigator. There is no standard language and many top crews have a system which is unique to them. Some people talk about bends in degrees (careful that degrees and speeds don't become confused), other talk about flat bends, easy bends, crests, etc. Avoid the use of words like 'slight' which could be confused with 'right'.

A further sophistication of pace notes are ice notes which may be used on snowy and icy stages. Just prior to the passage of the rally an experienced crew will pass over the stage, marking patches of ice and snow on copies of the notes—probably by underlining sections in red. These will then be passed to the team cars before they do the stage. The ice crews may also recommend the pattern of tyres to be used.

It is sometimes though that the dashboard on the navigator's side of the car should be covered with dials and clocks so that it looks like a scaled down version of Concorde's cockpit. This is not true; like everything else to do with navigation it is better to follow the old adage of "keep things simple".

PLEASE INDICATE TO WHICH ADDRESS CORRESPONDENCE SHOULD BE SENT

ENTRANT

☐ Name...

Address...

....Country...

Telephone...

Competition Licence No...Issued by...

FIRST DRIVER

☐ Surname [   ] Christian Name...

Address...

....Country...

Telephone...Nationality...

Competition Licence No...Issued by...

SECOND DRIVER

☐ Surname..Christian Name...

Address...

....Country...

Telephone...Nationality...

Competition Licence No...Issued by...

DETAILS OF CAR

Make...Model...

Class Entered...F.I.A. Homol. No...

Year of Manufacture...............................Cubic Capacity...

IF ANY REFUND OF ENTRY FEE HAS TO BE PAID, PLEASE INDICATE IF IT SHOULD BE PAID TO THE ENTRANT/FIRST DRIVER/SECOND DRIVER.

An entry form for a Lombard-R.A.C. Rally.

On a British road rally it is quite possible to succeed without any form of clock on the dashboard—a successful navigator may use his wrist watch (also a hand-held stop-watch if there are any sections timed to the second) as well as just a navigator's light and a map magnifier.

Every rally car should really have a flexible navigator's light fitted. There are numerous makes and there are different lengths to choose from. Select one that will suit your car and will reach across the map, which will be on your knee. Some people mount the lights on the gearbox housing or on the door, although this may be a bad thing as the light can easily be knocked off.

The flexible light is used mostly for map work when the car is stationary but if it has to be used when the car is mobile use one with an adjustable shade over the bulb so that it doesn't dazzle the driver. Always carry a spare bulb. The plug socket for the illuminated map magnifier should be fitted on the dashboard or gearbox housing.

Time and distance are important on stage rallies and you should have a clock, stopwatch and distance recorder. If you haven't got any of this equipment then go for the latest technology because the accuracy of quartz equipment is a navigator's dream. If you have more traditional equipment don't feel inferior—it will be perfectly adequate (provided you remember to keep the watches wound up of course). Any dash-mounted instruments should be properly lit.

Most top navigators wear a stopwatch on their wrist.

The Halda Tripmaster (with one trip) and the Twinmaster (not surprisingly with two) are widely used to measure distance and it is possible to alter their gearing so that they are accurate with different tyre sizes.

However, just as with watches, electronic devices are making great strides and the latest distance recorders driven by pulses generated by a non-driven road wheel (to cut out errors through wheel spin) are virtually miniature computers and really do make life easy; it is a very simple matter to set them to give completely accurate readings.

But ... a word of warning ladies and gentleman. Don't get so seduced by your advanced equipment that you forget that the rally will still be won by how well you and your driver perform, not by the gimmicks you have surrounded yourself with. The more you've spent on gadgetry, the bigger clown you are going to look when someone beats you using an egg-timer.

9 A rally diary

You might be forgiven for thinking that in order to take part successfully in a rally you have only three steps to take:

1) *Submit the entry to the organisers.*
2) *Prepare the car.*
3) *Get yourselves to the start by the appointed hour.*

These three things must all be done, of course, but there are many more steps to be taken before, during and after an event before you can say everything is under control.

The purpose of this chapter is to try to place the more important steps in order so that you can see the areas to which you should devote attention at various times. Professional teams have - or should have - every item organised down to the last detail with comprehensive books of crew movements, timetables and schedules. This ensures that everything runs smoothly and avoids last minute panics.

A crew that arrives at the start within minutes of their starting time, or one which has spent half the previous night on the telephone trying to locate an elusive service crew, or one that has had a last minute panic to find maps or tyres, is just not going to perform as well on an event as a well-organised crew. So ... get organised!

If the co-driver is doing his job properly, much of his duties will have been completed well before the start of the rally. In the case of private entries the driver will probably help in a lot of the pre-rally activities but for the purpose of this chapter let us assume that our co-driver is taking charge of *all* arrangements; we shall therefore address the reader in the role of co-driver. And although you will probably start on short events, near to where you live, we have covered a more elaborate event because the problems are greater.

So, let us suppose that you are planning to enter a one-day stage rally in Britain some hundred-and-fifty miles from home. These are some of the steps you should take prior to the event. We have shown them in a diary form for ease of reference. Many of the suggested timings are approximate and you may disagree with them; there are no hard and fast rules.

Incidentally, as a driver or co-driver, it is advisable to make some sort of planned competition programme for a full year (this helps budgeting) and to try to adhere to it as far as possible. Decide if you are going to tackle any local or major championships. Decide who does what before each event, so that you do not arrive in a town at midnight to find that you have no beds because each thought the other had made the bookings.

All of the following timings are calculated from the day of the rally!

Two months prior:

Write for regulations - organisers' addresses are usually shown in the motoring press. Study the regulations and ensure that the car is suitable for the event (in terms of preparation and homologation). Be sure that the crew has (or can obtain) suitable grades of competition licence.

As soon as possible after receiving the regulations:

Submit entry forms to organisers together with team entry form and service crew request forms (if applicable). Send the appropriate fee, preferably by cheque.

ADDITIONAL SUPPLEMENTARY REGULATIONS

1. The EAST BERKS MOTOR CLUB LIMITED will promote a Restricted permit rally on 7/8th January, 1978.

2. The meeting will be governed by the General Competition Rules, Standing Supplementary Regulations of the R.A.C. incorporating the provisions of the International Sporting Code of the F.I.A. these A.S.R.'s and any written instructions the promoting Club may issue for the event.

3. R.A.C. Permit Number: RAL/0701/1
   D.O.E. Authorisation Number: T.B.A.

4. The event is open to all fully elected members of the promoting club, ACSMC Road Rally Championship Contenders and members of the following invited clubs who have accepted an invitation in writing :-

   All ACSMC Member Clubs
   Bedford Motor Club
   Milton Keynes & District Motor Club
   Northampton & District Motor Club
   Three Counties Motor Club

   Club membership cards and competition licences will be inspected at signing-on.

5. The event is a round of the ACSMC Road Rally and Auto Club 159 Gold Star Rally Championships.

6. The event will start from Ford & Slater Limited, Aylesbury, M.R. 165/806146, and will finish in the Bicester area.

   Total mileage will be 190 miles on public roads. Scrutineering will begin at 20.00 hours, any competitors not signed-on by start time less 1 hour will be excluded. Individual times of scrutineering will be notified in the final instructions. Cars will start at 1 minute intervals the first leaving at 23.00 hours. The event will contain selective sections on the public roads which will run in accordance with the R.A.C.'s requirements.

   Map numbers 151, 152 and 165 metric will be required (latest editions).

   Cars will be identified by plates supplied by the organisers.

9. The maximum number of entries per class is 30 (except Masters). The minimum for each class is 5. The maximum entry for the meeting including reserves is 90. The minimum is 50. Should any of the minimum figures not be reached the Organisers have the right to cancel the meeting or amalgamate classes as required.

10. The entry list opens on publication of these regulations and closes finally on 31st December, 1977. The entry fee is £7.50. All entries must be made on official entry forms and accompanied by the appropriate fees. Entry fees will not be refunded after the closing date.

11. The Secretary of the Meeting is Graham Dore, 4 Southview Cottages, Shurlock Row, Reading, Berkshire. RG10 0PP Tel: Shurlock Row 480

    The Entries Secretary to whom all entries must be sent is Dave Ostler, 133 Hithercroft Road, Downley, High Wycombe, Bucks. Tel: High Wycombe 29849.

12. Other senior officials are listed at the front of these regulations.

13. Provisional results will be published by despatching a copy in writing by post within seven days of the event. Protests must be made in accordance with S.S.R. P47 (b).

14. Entrants will be supplied with a Road Book and Time Card at signing-on. Route cards will be issued at various controls during the event. These documents will provide all the information necessary to enable competitors to comply with S.S.R. (S36).

15. All other S.S.R.'s of the R.A.C. apply as written except for the following which are modified:-

    P40   – Competitors may be members of more than one Team.
    P43   – See A.S.R. 7.
    S17   – All 'stop' 'no' and 'Q' boards are mandatory.
    S35   – Unspecified checks may be established.
    S45   – Timing over certain sections of the route will be to an accuracy of less than 1 minute.
    S47   – Official time pieces will be used by Marshals.
    S50   – Controls will open 15 minutes before due time of the first car and close 30 minutes after due time of last car.
    S58   – All competitors must re-start the control after fuel halts on scheduled time.
    S59   – Details will be given in road books/route cards of penalty free make-up time.
    S64   – See A.S.R. 16
    S66   – The fail system of marking will be used, modified as follows :-

    (a) to (d)   – 1 Fail

    (e) to (k) and (s) – Delete

    (l) Departure from a time control before due time – 2 points per minute.

    (m) Arriving at a time control after corrected time – 1 point per minute. $^1/60$ point per second on sections timed to an accuracy of less than 1 minute.

Two pages of regulations for a typical 'Restricted' road rally.

EAST BERKS MOTOR CLUB LIMITED   ENTRY FORM   PLEASE USE BLOCK CAPITALS

OAKLEAF Rally 7/8th JANUARY 1978

ENTRANT:

Name: .... Address.....................
Comp. Licence No: ....

N.B. Entrants name will NOT appear on the entry list unless their Competition Licence number is show above.

DRIVER:

Name: .... Address.....................
Comp. Licence No: ....
Club: ....
ACSMC Contender* YES/NO .... Tel : ....
RDS Proposal form required* YES/NO RDS Number: ....
Own Insurers (if applicable) : Name.....................
                                 Address.....................
                                 ....

NAVIGATOR:

Name: .... Address.....................
Comp. Licence No: ....
Club: ....
ACSMC Contender* YES/NO .... Tel : ....

CAR:

Make: .... Model: .... Colour: ....
Capacity...........cc OHC/Push Rod*   Reg. No: ....

CLASS ENTERED: 2/ 3/ 4/ 5/ 6/ 7/ 8/ 9/ 10

I enclose cheque / postal order / cash for:-   Entry Fee   £ 7.50
(PLEASE MAKE ALL CHEQUES PAYABLE TO: RDS Insurance *£ 6.00
EAST BERKS MOTOR CLUB LIMITED)
N.B. POST DATED CHEQUES WILL NOT BE ACCEPTED   £

Please give results of 1977 road rallies for seeding information:-

Please return this completed form to the Entries Secretary, Dave Ostler at:
133 Hithercroft Road, Downley, High Wycombe, Bucks. Tel: H.W. 29849

* Please delete as applicable

A straightforward entry form.

EAST BERKS MOTOR CLUB LTD.   OAKLEAF RALLY   7/8 JANUARY 1978

ENTRY LIST

No.	Entrant / Driver / Navigator	Car	Class	Reg No	Colour	Club
1.	Entrant: McGill Automotive/Northampton & Dist.C.C. Graham Parker/Nigel Evans	Kadett GTE	1	MOY217P	Yellow/Black	North'ton
2.	Entrant: Aylesbury Motor Club Roland Shepherd/Mike Wise	Escort RS	1	TWK400M	Blue	Aylesbury
3.	Bill Harrap/Peter Rushforth	Escort RS	1	RTM128M	Blue	Aylesbury/ Craven
4.	Entrant: Craven Motor Club Derek Looker/Jim Bowie	Anglia	1	8179 PJ	White	Craven
5.	Entrant: Ripspeed Racing International Ken Hutton/John Hill	Avenger	1	NYL678L	Yellow/Black	Brent Vale
6.	Mike Hickman/Geoff Richards	Escort TC	1	DOU120K	Red	Mid Thames
7.	Entrant: Chiltern Car Club Malcolm Anderson/Roland Carlin	Imp Sport	1	GRX495K	Red/Yellow	AC159
8.	Entrant: Tylers Green Motor Club Dick Mauger/Dick Steptoe	Mexico	1	HAK461L	White/Blue	Aylesbury
9.	Entrant: Henley Plastics Injection Moulders Dot Warne/Dave Sales	Escort RS	1	LMJ928P	Red/Yellow	Craven
10.						
11.	Entrant: Croydon & Dist. Motor Club Ltd. Derek Lavender/Martin Quaintance	Ford Mascot	2	MHV373P	White	Croydon
12.	Dave Large/Paul Maynard	Cortina Mk1	3	RGC184E	White	Hampton
13.	Ian Donaldson/Martin Wyeth	Escort RS	2	LKH154P	Blue/White	Craven
14.	Entrant: Winchester & Dist. Car Club David Clarke/Peter Harwood	Cooper S	4	DUY600B	Blue	Winchester
15.	Entrant: East Berks M.C./Chiltern C.C. Keith Rumary/Phil Markham	Avenger	2		Blue	AC159
16.	Tom Stoate/Walter Mew	Escort RS	1	CLA373H	Brown/Gold	Craven/ Bracknell
17.	Entrant: P.North T.Wyeth/P.North	Escort	3	XPA130G	White	Portals
18.	Ron Lee/Jon Quelon	Escort	3	UWL870K	Yellow	Witney
19.	Peter Johnson/Donald Fowler	Escort TC	2	EPK226J	Maize	Mid Thames
20.	Paul Adams/Pete Twite	Chevette	4	PET398R	Red	Hampton
21.	Entrant: Craven Motor Club Dick Vaughan/Ian Fisher	Avenger	4	EUR783K	Yellow	Craven
22.	Tom Lambert/Fiona Lambert	Escort RS	2	HRG672H	Yellow	Hampton
23.	Milton Keynes & Dist. Motor Club Dave Havard/G.Waller	Escort	4	WKX607M	White	M.Keynes
24.	Entrant: Craven Motor Club M.Pearson-Kirk/John King	MGBGT	2	HUD578N	White	Craven
25.	Mick Connell/Chris White	Escort	3	WLF197N	Green/White	Craven
26.	Bob Mole/Pete Stedman	Escort	3	MJW156P	Green/White	Craven
27.	Nick Beare/Richard Allmutt	Avenger	3	RRD586M	White	Mid Thames/ AC159
28.	Entrant: Newbury Express Panelcraft Dave Toomey/Rich Walker	TR7	2	NMO290R	White/Blue	Craven
29.	Entrant: Team 218WO Colin Short/John Phillips	Manta SR	2	KPL416P	Black	ACSMC
30.	Entrant: Middlesex County A.C. Jim Olney/Jerry Shapley	Escort	3		Red	Middx.Co.
31.	Joe Adams/Tony Hutchinson	California	4	4KO	Silver	Bedford
32.	J.Lake/J.Bromfield	Davrian	4	LBL333P	Blue	East Berks
33.	Entrant: Bedford Motor Club Mike Newton/Rod Botteley	Avenger	4	HDU402L	White	Bedford
34.	Entrant: Farnborough & Dist. Motor Club Jim Morris/I.Cooper	Escort	4	SRX651G	Red	Farnborough NatWest
35.	Entrant: VMRCMS C.Ellis/B.Riley	Escort RS	2	HPT3N	Yellow/Orange	AC159
36.	Entrant: Tylers Green Motor Club Ltd. Chris Coxall/Mike Crockett	Viva	4	TMD433E	Blue/Green	AC159
37.	Mike Downie/Dave Parkinson	Dolomite	2	MTS980H	Yellow	Bedford

'Runners and riders' for the same rally.

Study the regulations to find the location of start, half way and finish, and decide how many (if any) hotel rooms you will require. Many rally organisers specify the hotel to be used as rally headquarters and often list other suitable hotels. Some even list hotel room rates and might include official booking forms with the regulations. It is quite common for organisers to negotiate special rates with hoteliers.

It helps the efficiency of a team if all personnel are housed at a convenient place prior to the rally. The most suitable hotels fill quickly - book early.

By the way, if all this sounds a bit grandiose and expensive, well, nobody should kid themselves that motor sport is cheap. However if the cost of hotels frightens you, try bed and breakfast places - or perhaps a caravan or tent.

If possible avoid driving a long way just before the start of a rally – you may save a lodging bill but you may not perform at 100% efficiency because of fatigue.

Try to discover from the regulations the types of stages and whether any practice is necessary or allowed (for the purpose of this exercise we will assume that there is no practice, therefore your entourage will travel to the rally just one day before the start). The organisers will probably advise you of stage surfaces; if there is any doubt from the regulations telephone the organisers who may give you a little more information without actually revealing details of the route.

Discuss with your driver the mechanical and tyre requirements. Ensure that tyres of the right type are ordered. Have enough spare wheels.

Make sure that any parts needed for the car are available or ordered in good time and work out a car preparation programme. Some things are going to need replacing at given intervals - it makes sense to order them well in advance.

Sort out a service crew, though *only* if one is allowed. Make a detailed check list of the parts and tools they must carry - works service crews have detailed lists of everything down to the last washer. Allow time for proper maintenance work to be carried out on the service car itself - it often gets forgotten.

EAST BERKS MOTOR CLUB LTD OAKLEAF RALLY 19

SPECTATOR INFORMATION.

Once again the Oakleaf is here and hopefully it will be as troublefree as in previous years. However we rely on spectators to a great extent not to antagonise the general public as it is difficult for those not involved in the sport to differentiate between spectators and competing cars, so don't upset anybody, drive consideratel and keep the noise down at spectator points. Some of thes points are within earshot of peoples homes and bearing in mind that sound carries further at night don't shout to one another along the road.

Listed below there are nine spectator points. If you approach the spectator point as indicated from the nearest A or B road avoiding the roads so specified for rally use you should avoid the rally on minor roads.

We wish you a good nights spectating,

PR Officer, Oakleaf '78.

Grid Ref.	Car 1 Due approx	Spectators App.& Dept
165/E712210S	23.10	West
165,152/SW 648 312 SE	23.35	North East
165,152/NE 740345 NNW	23.50	South West
152/ NW668 356 ENE	00.20	South
First Petrol- Please avoid Farthinghoe.		
152/ S545 419W	01.15	South East, yellow to Brackley.
151/ SE514 487WSW	01.30	North
151/ NE374 392SE	02.11	South West
Second Petrol- Hartwells of Banbury.		
151/ SSE306425WSW	03.50	North
151/ NW343309NE	04.20	South

Rallies attract spectators and it is important that they do not annoy non-enthusiasts – hence sheets like this.

STOP JUNCTIONS

A	765 190
B	690¾ 190
C	673½ 154
D	653½ 198 (also DIP headlights)
E	661 328¾
F	710½ 317
G	737½ 332
H	765¼ 335 (also DIP headlights)
I	733½ 361½
J	675 349
K	613 332
L	557 357
M	529 362
N	518½ 439¾
O	485 455½
P	499¼ 488¾
Q	444¾ 474¼
R	412½ 510
S	384 520
T	409 417
U	417½ 377
V	365¼ 375¾
W	261 404
X	285½ 373¾
Y	355 349
Z	

The following stop junctions coincide with Time controls. You will be deemed to have stopped at the junction as soon as you have been signed in.

648 226	574¾ 330½	530¼ 367½
376¾ 490½	366¼ 461¾	430 435
370½ 378½	320¾ 426	263½ 371¾
362 302½	390½ 402	

NOTE: DO NOT stop at the following junction.

535¼ 419½ (Road conditions permitting)

As stated in the final instructions 'Stop Controls' will be in operation at some stop junctions. These should be treated similarly to passage controls; however cars must come to a standstill as near as possible to the white give-way lines on the road and when signed in are free to drive straight off-provided nothing is coming of course! The procedure is the same at Time Controls sited at stop junctions. Other stop junctions will be observed in the usual way.

A key sheet for the co-driver to mark on his map.

A competitor signs in at the start.

Order Ordnance Survey maps for yourself and the service crew, as well as $\frac{1}{4}$ inch maps or other small scale road maps for the service crew who will not need detailed maps for the whole route (petrol company maps are often quite adequate).

One or two weeks prior:

Receive final regulations from organisers. These will spell out any extra requirements. Possibly additional maps, scrutineers' requirements and more details about the rally will be given in the final regulations. Some route details and instructions about timing, arrowing and service crew arrangements will be given.

Above all, the final regulations will tell you where to start, when to start and what time and where you must report for scrutineering. An entry list will be included and you will see the number allocated to your car. You will probably be given individual reporting times for scrutineering. Incidentally, if you don't like your starting number there is very little you can do about it. *Don't* ring the organisers bewailing the fact that your position is too low in the list and that you ought to be ahead of Fred Bloggs as you beat him on the last event. The organisers will be far too busy to listen to your twittering.

The driver must be told of any changes notified in the final regulations. Many people get caught out with things that have not been done through not noticing changes. Fire extinguisher requirements, the permanent fixing of tip-forward driving seats, fireproofing, spotlights, etc. are often mentioned in this context.

Let your driver know the salient details of the rally. Let him know the time that you and the service crew must leave home, and the time that it will take to get to the start. Distances of the rally etc. are also important. Don't fill his head with too much or else he will forget the more important points. If you haven't received confirmation of hotel bookings, check with the hotel that all is in order. There is nothing like a rally for throwing hotel reservation desks into chaos.

Make sure that the car is beginning to look as though it will make the start line. Make sure that any parts which were expected to arrive have been delivered. If not, go for them.

As soon as possible, your driver should be testing the car. He should be making sure that everything is to his liking. On the way to the start cover a few miles briskly on a quiet road just to finally shake-down you and the car.

EAST BERKS MOTOR CLUB LIMITED   OAKLEAF RALLY   7/8th JANUARY, 19?

SCRUTINEERING CARD

No: ....   CLASS: ....

DRIVER ....   NAVIGATOR ....

LICENCE NO: ....   LICENCE NO: ....

ENTRANTS LICENCE NO: ....   CLUB CARDS ....
                                     R.D.S. ACCEPTANCE
R.D.S. NO: ....   INSPECTED SIGNATURE....................

OTHER INSURANCE ....

OTHER INSURANCE INSPECTED SIGNATURE ....

CAR REG. NO: .... COLOUR .... MODEL ....

TYRES (Road Legal) ....

DIPPING SPOTS WITH HEADS.....................   ....

SIDE LIGHTS, FLASHERS ....

TAIL & STOP LIGHTS ....

REVERSE LIGHTS/WARNING ....

WIPERS, WASHERS ....

STEERING PLAY ....

BRAKE PEDAL TRAVEL ....

SEAT BELTS ....

SEATS SECURE ....

BATTERY SECURE ....

NO LOOSE FUEL CANS ....

WARNING TRIANGLE ....

OTHERS ....

BODY DAMAGE (note if any) ....

....

SCRUTINEERS SIGNATURE ....

NOISE SCRUTINEER SIGNATURE .... 1st.

                           .... 2nd.

DAMAGE DECLARATION:- (to be completed by Crew at finish)
        DAMAGE   M.R. OF INCURRENCE

N.B. For non-finishers - this card   SIGNATURE OF DRIVER
must be returned to the Secretary of
the Meeting within 7 days of the event.   ....

                                          SIGNATURE OF SCRUTINEER

A typical scrutineering card.

EAST BERKS MOTOR CLUB   OAKLEAF RALLY   197

ROUTE OF LINK SECTIONS AND SELECTIVES

Link sections to be traversed quietly on dipped lights.

1) Link from start to TC1 at SSE 787½ 167. Use gates
    on yellow, not cattle grids.

2) TC10in at S648 226E, then via S653½233W to TC10 out
    at S648237½ .

3) TC14 in at N678¼333 to TC14out at W690 317 .

4) TC19in at ENE719348½ to TC19out at W690317 .

5) TC26in at E533 361½ to TC26out at E521363 .

6) TC28in at SSW535½393¾ to Petrol at SE537¾397NW.
    Please be very quiet and do not block the pumps as
    this is only a lengthened link section to enable
    you to take on petrol. Then to TC28out at S542408.

7) TC30in at S528442; proceed to SS1 at S527¾444.
    Queue south of B road, only cross when it is your
    turn to start the selective. Selective route via
    527½447WNW to Selective Finish at E500456.

    Then link via 485456 (very quiet Upper Wardington
    and Wardington) to Start Selective 2 at W495470.
    Finish Selective 2 at E505488½ .

    Then link (very quiet Chipping Warden) to Start
    Selective 3 at SE491491½. Finish Selective 3 at
    E446475 .

    Then link (very quiet Mollington) to TC30out at
    ENE434473 .

    The sections between selective finishes and starts
    are link sections and should be traversed QUIETLY.

8) TC37in at WNW3644?0 to TC37out at NE378½400 .

9) TC40in at SW430435, via W455418 to petrol at
    Hartwells (453?414). Hand in completed Time Cards
    to the marshal as on attached diagram. Then link
    to TC40out at ESE431369 .

10) TC51in at SW300½363½ to TC51out at W303372 .

11) TC 59 to finish - details on preplot route section.

More route instructions.

EAST BERKS M.C. LTD   OAKLEAF RALLY 7/8 JAN. 197:   TIME CARD 1

CREW					No.

T.C.	MAKE UP TIME	TIME	SIGNATURE	COMMENTS	OFFICIAL USE ONLY
1	-				
2	-				
3	-				
4	-				
5	-				
6	-				
7	-				
8	-				
9	-				
10 IN	6 mins				
10 OUT	-				
11	-				
12	-				
STOP					

A Time Card covering twelve controls. The co-driver should guard it with his life!

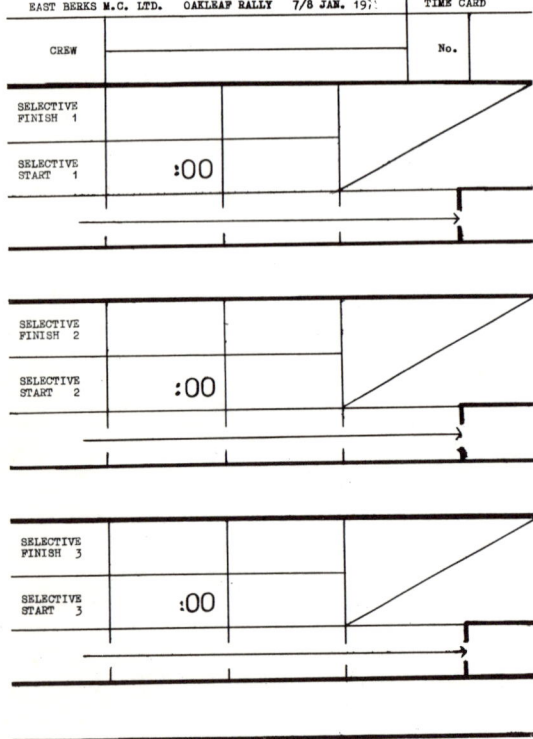

EAST BERKS M.C. LTD.   OAKLEAF RALLY 7/8 JAN. 197:   TIME CARD

CREW			No.

SELECTIVE FINISH 1

SELECTIVE START 1   :00

SELECTIVE FINISH 2

SELECTIVE START 2   :00

SELECTIVE FINISH 3

SELECTIVE START 3   :00

TOTAL PENALTY:

A Special Stage Time Card covering three selectives. Note that each stage will be started on a 'whole' minute.

EAST BERKS M.C.   OAKLEAF RALLY   JAN 7/8 1978

HANDOUT 6   TC 7 — TC 10 IN COMPETITIVE

NE   655¾   147½   N
WSW 661   177¾   N
ESE   636½   200   NNE   TO TC 10 IN

THEN LINK TO TC 10 OUT;   QUIET MARSH GIBBON

EAST BERKS M.C.   OAKLEAF RALLY   JAN 7/8 1978

HANDOUT 10   TC 19 OUT — TC 21 COMPETITIVE

(junction route symbols)

(junction route symbols)   TO TC 21

EAST BERKS M.C. OAKLEAF RALLY   JAN 7/8 1978

HANDOUT 14   TC 28 OUT TO SECOND PETROL
COMPETITIVE VIA:

(junction route symbols)

TO TC 30 IN AND VIA SELECTIVES 1, 2, AND 3   TO TC 30 OUT

THEN COMPETITIVE VIA:

ESE   417¼   478   NNE
SW   431   495½   NNW
E   384   519¾   SSE
NE   376¾   490½   SE
N   354   431¼   E

TO TC 37 IN. THEN LINK, QUIET TO TC 37 OUT

THEN COMPETITIVE VIA:
WNW   387½   385½

141   115   158   157 NNE

(junction route symbols)   TO TC 40 IN.

THEN LINK TO PETROL; QUIET BANBURY.

On this road rally co-drivers were kept on their toes and had to cope with route instructions handed out in several different ways – these are just three of the sheets given out. Note the detailed directions of approach and departure specified with map references.

Day prior:

Arrive in good time for scrutineering. Rally scrutineers sometimes tuck themselves away in back street garages which may be difficult to find. Make sure that the crash helmets are with the car for scrutineering (not in your hotel bedroom). Check if you have to report to Rally Headquarters within a specified time after leaving scrutineering - if so, keep an eye on this as you can be penalised for being late.

Go with your driver to signing on. Take your competition licences (and Entrant's licence if necessary) and anything else that final regulations ask you to show (possibly club membership cards or insurance certificates).

Collect road books, time cards or whatever else is issued. Collect service crew paperwork if required. Check that you have every page of every document as well as any amendment sheets. Have a look at rally noticeboards for any last-minute amendments, particularly route alterations.

Make sure you know who's who in the Organising team. Make a note of the room number of the Clerk of the Course for possible bribing (we're only joking). Make a note of room numbers of any desirable female members of the organising team (if you navigate for some Finns they will count this as key information!).

Now return to your hotel and plot the route on your maps. It is advisable to do this by yourself in perfect peace although some drivers help by reading out references. When plotted, check everything and ensure that black spots, out-of-bounds areas and service points have been marked.

Now it will probably be your lot to plot the service crew's route too. Many people (including works teams) write a simple service schedule and hand the list of references and times to the service crew so that they can plot their own itinerary. Part of the fun of amateur servicing is that you almost take part in little rallies of your own - but don't get so carried away in your driving that you become a nuisance, either to the rally or other motorists.

Always set a sensible average speed schedule for your service crew. Mechanics have been injured because of stupid service schedules - a heavily laden service car is not the best vehicle to drive quickly on twisty roads.

Make sure that your service stops are marked up in your road book and on your map. The service crew *must* be advised of any out-of-bounds areas (organisers will often specify certain roads as prohibited to service crews to avoid annoyance or congestion).

Allow time for a service meeting with your crew - you must check their maps. They need to know where and when you need tyres and fuel.

Incidentally, when leaving rally and service cars parked overnight make sure that as much as possible is locked away. Sadly, stuff does get pinched - even more ghoulishly things even get stolen from cars which have crashed and been abandoned on stages.

Hopefully you and your service crew will find time to eat before the rally but do not waste valuable plotting time on a four-course meal - order sandwiches and coffee in your room if there is any chance of running out of time.

Make sure your driver is not sampling the local brew too enthusiastically and tell him what time he has to get up. Try to send him to bed at a reasonable time and tell him to restrict any love-making sessions to about four hours. Service crews should also be told what time to book a call for.

Take another trip to Rally Headquarters, just to make sure that there are no alterations. On an Italian San Remo Rally a few years ago the organisers changed the starting time and more than one experienced competitor appeared at the start when the rally had left!

Finally, book early morning calls and go to bed. But *always* take your own alarm clock. The chaos caused by rallies in the reservations areas can also spread to the early morning call department, as many competitors know to their cost.

Day of rally:

Get up, get dressed (we'll spare you the ablutionary details) and collect together all necessary documents, ignition keys, crash helmets and if supplied (a very important item) the start card. Many organisers issue a start card at scrutineering which must be produced before you can start the rally.

Be at your car in good time, at least fiteen minutes before the start; many rally cars are the very devil to start on a cold, icy morning after a night in an exposed car park.

During the rally you should keep a detailed note of stage times together with other competitors' times. Don't blab too much to other competitors but keep a running total of all the times and compare them with the organisers whenever they publish a list. You will often find intermediate results displayed at main controls during the event. If these times and yours do not agree, do not get in too much of a tizzy as there are often mistakes in these results, which are usually telephoned through from Rally Headquarters and presented simply as a guide.

Rally results sheet — penalty marks per control.

CAR	CLASS	TC →	2	3	4	5	6	7	8	9	10 IN	10 OUT	11	12	13	14 IN	14 OUT	15	16	17	18	19 IN	19 OUT	20	21	22	23	24	25	26 IN	26 OUT	27	28 IN	28 OUT	29 IN	30 OUT	SEL.1	SEL.2	30 cut	31	32	33	34	35	36	37
85	8		2	3	2	1	–	4	2	1	–	1	–	2	2	2	–	2	2	–	2	5	3	–	2	–	3	2	F	F	–	F	F	–	F	F	2-29	3-04	F F F F F		–	–			
86	8		1	3	2	1	1	3	1	–	1	–	1	–	1	2	–	2	–	1	–	3	2	4	–	2	–	.)	–	1	–	1	–	1	–	1	–	2-33	3-10	4E 1 – 2 1 – 1						
87	9		3	3	1	2	1	4	–	1	–	1	–	2	RETIRED																									RETIRED						
88	7		2	2	1	3	–	3	–	1	–	1	–	2	1	2	–	1	2	–	2	2	3	–	1	–	2	3	–	1	–	1	–	1	–											
89	8		3	2	1	2	–	3	1	2	–	1	2	–	1	2	–	2	2	–	3	–	5	–	2	–	3	–	1	–	2	–	3	–	1	–	2	6-08	3-35	F F F F F F						
90	9		3	2	3	2	3	–	4	1	–	1	–	5	1	3	F	–	F	–	F	RETIRED																									

ADDITIONAL PENALTIES & EXPLANATIONS

F = FAIL FOR OTL OR NOT VISITING CONTROL EXCEPT AS FOLLOWS:

CAR 35: 1F AT TC 37 BUT FOR NOT COMPLYING WITH LINK SECTION REQUIREMENTS.

CARS 45, 76, 84: 1F FOR NOT STOPPING AT STOP JUNCTION.

CAR 52: 1F AT TC 37 IN. FOR W.D.A.

CAR 69: 1F AT TC 19 IN FOR W.D.A./TURNING ROUND IN CONTROL/VISITING CONTROL TWICE.

DNF DENOTES NON FINISHER - FAILED TO VISIT FINAL CONTROL WITHIN 30 MINS LATENESS

E DENOTES LEAVING CONTROL EARLY OR MAKING UP TIME IN THE WRONG PLACES

The rally doesn't end at the finishing line – the results should be studied to see if the organisers' marks agree with yours – but DO NOT become a barrack room lawyer trying to win rallies by post-rally protests. Note the explanation of "F". "W.D.A." means wrong direction of approach.

Apart from the usual navigational duties, (covered in detail elsewhere) allow yourself the luxury of a glance at the awards page in the regulations if you think you might be in with a chance, but this should be at a very late stage in the rally, probably on the run in. Many superstitious co-drivers refuse to look at that page until the car is locked up at the finish!

A good co-driver will be totalling his penalties on the run-in to the finish so that he is ready to check the totals when official results are announced. Make sure the car is left where it should be, i.e. in the finish compound; if there is any likelihood of winning a major or class award then it may have to be scrutineered for eligibility (this happens mostly on Internationals).

When you re-enter the hotel/rally headquarters keep the driver away from the bar for a while - radio interviews with winners (well you *may* have won) don't sound so good with slurred speech.

As soon as the results are announced you should check them with your records. Make sure they tally. If there is a figure with which you disagree you should check with the Organisers to see if it is their mistake or yours. Stay within reach of the results room (stages are often cancelled or reinstated and this can alter the results dramatically). If your times do not agree, or if you do not agree with one of the Organisers' decisions regarding a cancelled or reinstated stage, don't start shouting and protesting too readily. By all means, check with the Organisers and make your point but study your case *very* carefully before considering protesting. *If* you feel very badly done by, then you may feel you *have* to protest but *please don't* become a barrack room lawyer bickering and protesting about trivialties. The place to win rallies is in the car.

If you look like winning, then make sure that you and your driver know where the presentation is to be held. Make sure that your driver goes to it; it is not unknown for winning drivers to be missing when awards are presented. This is the height of bad manners; you owe it to Organisers, spectators, fellow competitors and marshals to be there. If you win, you will probably be expected to make a speech. Be succinct and genuine. You will not be expected to be witty or particularly eloquent, but obey some protocol - if there are Mayors, Lordships or whatever else present, then start your speech properly. Always thank the Club, the organisers and marshals, whatever your personal feelings. Never knock other competitors and try to appear as humble as possible without overdoing it.

Your work is now over, and you can let all those regulations, figures and numbers fade into oblivion. You may now find their place taken by more useful numbers - like the phone number of that lady you met at signing on ...

10 How to organise a rally

If you want a really thankless task, organise a rally. You will spend hundreds of hours in hard, tiring and frustrating work, only to have your results greeted with last-minute disappointments, abuse and possibly even protests.

However, we mustn't deter potential rally organisers because the sport literally depends on competent, efficient enthusiasts prepared to undertake the work.

One chapter in a book of this size can hardly offer a complete guide for organisers, but it can highlight most of the important steps to be taken when organising a rally. Remember, as the organiser of an average Restricted rally you will be catering for a hundred or more of the most agile minds in the sport, and they'll be ready to pounce on any small loophole that presents itself. So you must be on your toes from the moment you start to lay plans for a rally.

It would be unwise for a club to give the sole responsibility for organising an event to a complete beginner. Far more sensible to let a person gain experience by allowing him to understudy an established organiser before taking the reins himself.

Probably the first thing to look at from a club's point of view is the *reason* for running a rally. It is no good running a rally as a means of swelling club funds, or as a means of putting a club on the map. Probably the main reason for running a rally will be to help complete the club's calendar and give members a varied and full year of motor sport.

Having decided to run a rally, the club must decide whether to run a stage or road event. Numerous factors will have a bearing on the decision but the most likely will be the availability and type of terrain in which the club finds itself. Another guiding factor will be the relative popularity of the two types of event.

Although it must be the aim of every organiser to run a perfect rally with no mistakes, perfect events are few and far between. Even some of the world's major rallies make mistakes in regulations or paperwork. After all there are a thousand-and-one things for an organiser of a rally to remember; nevertheless, every organiser should strive for perfection.

A club will need a small team or committee of people to organise an event, the size of the team depending on the size and nature of the rally. Generally speaking, stage rallies require greater manpower and are probably more difficult for the beginner to organise although the organiser of a road rally may meet his share of problems during the route authorisation stage, unless he is very lucky.

However, assuming that you are going to organise a road rally, fix the date and duration of the event. Selecting the date can be difficult; it is no good running a rally if it is going to clash with another event on the same night. If the route clashes in the same area then you will not be able ro run your rally, and if the event clashes with one in a different area, then you will probably not attract entries. So great care must be taken in selecting a suitable date.

It will be necessary to apply for a date through your local Regional Association's "dates meeting". Most of the better established rallies have a traditional date, so if you plan to use the same area keep away from their dates. You must keep six weeks away from any club running in your patch.

Naturally an organiser must have a good idea of the time of year he plans to run the rally. Some of the factors that might influence a date choice are the hours of darkness at a given time of year, the condition of unsurfaced tracks during different seasons or any regional peculiarities, like the presence of holiday-makers.

At a very early stage you will have to decide on the area in which you plan to run the rally, bearing in mind most of the best rally territory is already well spoken for. It is best to run a rally in your own area if

APPLICATION FOR A RALLY PERMIT

(In accordance with RAC Standing Supplementary Regulations, Sections P & S)

DOT Authorisation is not required before submitting an application permit.

TO BE SUBMITTED IN ACCORDANCE WITH PARAGRAPHS C12 AND C22 OF THE RAC REGULATIONS FOR THE ORGANISATION OF MOTOR COMPETITIONS.
Application for Events Qualifying for Exemption to G.C.R.'s C23/24 need not be submitted on this form.

In order to economise within the R.A.C. and reduce the amount of time wasted in reading through Regulations the R.A.C. has devised this system of permit application. It provides all the information necessary to complete the A.S.R.'s but still allows organisers to include such information as may be deemed necessary to the individual event after the main Regulations have been explained.

Name of Organising Club(s) ....

.... Date of the Event.................................

Status .... D.O.T. Authorisation No. .... (if known)

As Secretary of the Meeting I undertake on behalf of the Club(s) organising this Competition that it will be conducted in accordance with the General Competition Rules, Standing Supplementary Regulations and other requirements of the R.A.C., and the Additional Supplementary Regulations overleaf (in addition to the Motor Vehicles (Competitions and Trials) Regulations).

Signature .... Date........................ Name ....

Phone No. .... Home   Address ....

No. ....Business   ....

Please place tick in appropriate column

If any answer to questions 1 to 6 is NO, please refer to the Organisation of Motor Competitions before forwarding application.

	YES	NO
1. Has your Club a date in the R.A.C. Fixture List for this event? (C2)		
2. Has your Club promoted a rally of this status before? (C10)		
4. Have you received a written acceptance from all the co-promoting/invited Clubs? (C11)		
5. Is the event subject to authorisation under D.O.T. Regulations?		
If NO, explain why not		
6. Do you understand that **ALL** events on the public highway are subject to the standard conditions laid down in the Motor Vehicles (Competition & Trials) Regulations?		
7. Are there any special stages? (C90) (Note special Vehicle Regulations) .		
If YES, how many?...............................		
8. Are there any selective sections? (C89)		
9. Is proof of permission from all Landowners of Special stages enclosed?		
12. Is this a qualifying round for any Championship? (C25)		
If YES, specify which Championships		
13. Have the requirements of C88 been complied with?		

NOTE: No fees should be forwarded with this application. The R.A.C. and Insurance rates will be advised with the acknowledgement of the application.

Organising a rally is a demanding business. This is just part of the application form for a Rally Permit.

possible as this makes the marshalling and route work much easier and, in any case, clubs in other areas won't thank you if you invade their area and upset the natives, the police or anyone else.

Among all the other decisions to be made at an early stage will be that of the status of the event. Obviously, novice organisers should start off on twelve car or "closed-to-club" rallies while an experienced team should be able to cope with a closed-joint or Restricted event. Generally speaking, the bigger the event, the better the standard of entry and therefore the more demanding and critical their requirements.

No rally can be run legally unless the event is 'approved'. The only events that do not have to conform to the Motor Vehicles (Competition and Trials) Regulations, 1969, are 1) events with not more than twelve vehicles, 2) events where there is no route and where competitors are not timed or required to visit places other than a finish venue, 3) road safety events and 4) military training exercises (we know some rally cars are built like tanks - some even handle like them - but they still don't fall in this category).

Assuming that your event requires authorisation then it will be necessary for you to study the statutory regulations and complete the appropriate application forms. These are available from the R.A.C. British Motor Sports Council, 31 Belgrave Square, London SW1X 8QH (01-235-8601) and from the Royal Scottish Automobile Club, 11 Blytheswood Square, Glasgow (041-221-3850).

Before submitting the application and route for authorisation you must make contact with numerous organisations. The Regional Associations of car clubs play a useful role in co-ordinating lists of road information and can often save many wasted hours by giving advice on certain areas to avoid; putting your route through some of these areas can mean almost certain refusal from the rally authorisation department.

If your route goes anywhere near a National Park it is necessary to contact the National Park Officer. It is advisable to contact the National Farmers' Union and, of course, the police. Although the R.A.C. will send details of your event to the police in your area, it is sensible to make an approach before the application is made as you can again save a lot of time by avoiding areas to which they are likely to object.

After these informal approaches have been cleared, you are ready to submit your application for authorisation. Read Schedule 3 of the Statutory Regulations to make sure that your event complies fully with them. There are seventeen separate standard conditions which the event must fulfil, most of which concern the routing and timing of the event. If the event does not comply with the standard conditions then the organiser and competitors can face a fine of £50 under Section 36 of the Road Traffic Act 1962.

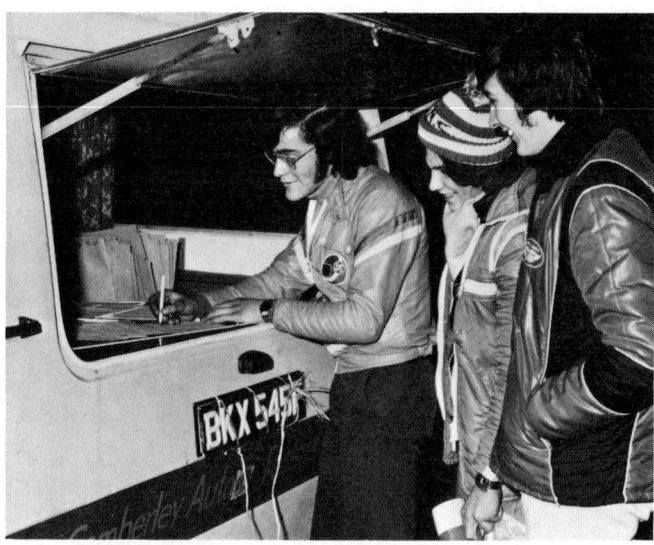

Without marshals there wouldn't be any rallying. Here a group of stalwarts sign on for a hard night's work. Note the envelopes ready packed with marshals' instructions.

Signs of the times.

When the application form is sent in to the authority, two copies of a tracing from the appropriate 1-50,000 scale Ordnance Survey Map (quarter inch O.S. map in the case of Scotland) must also be submitted. The tracings must contain full details of the route together with details of timing and controls. It will also be necessary to send a fee which is based on the mileage of the rally (details are shown in the application literature). Most of the fee, which can range from approximately £20 to £60, will be returned should the event not be authorised.

It may seem unnecessary to submit an application six months before an event but it can take a long time to gain authorisation, particularly if there are any route clashes when the R.A.C. will suggest re-routes and tracings will fly back and forth between authorisers and organisers.

Scrutineering will often be more for safety than homologation purposes. Here at the start of the Oakleaf Rally scrutineers check lights...

In addition to the *application* fee already mentioned it will be necessary to pay an *authorisation* fee should your event be given the green light. This is based on the number of vehicles taking part and upon the length of event. It can range from 75 pence to £3 per vehicle. An R.A.C. recognised club will also require an R.A.C. permit. Once a club is recognised by the R.A.C. it agrees to be bound by rules and regulations that are laid down in the R.A.C. Motorsport Regulations and updated each year in their Year Book. The Year Book deals with all forms of motor sport and has a section purely devoted to rallies where requirements and standard conditions are laid down. The R.A.C. permit provides Third Party legal liability insurance and should be applied for some six weeks or so before the event. The fees for this are again based on a *per capita* basis.

Talking about insurance, remember that most private insurance policies no longer give cover for rallies and so the R.A.C's brokers have devised a scheme whereby individuals can obtain road traffic cover for the duration of an event. The administration of this insurance must be done through the organising club and the brokers issue a block cover note for the event. The R.A.C. will give details of this insurance, together with another policy which insures officials during an event (providing they have all signed a special form).

... engines ...

... and seat mountings.

In the previous paragraphs we have implied that the event to be organised is a road rally; certainly these can be more complicated in the authorisation application stages. Similar procedures will have to be followed by the organisers of a stage rally although there will, of course, need to be more liaison with individual land-owners. Permission from land-owners will have to be submitted to the authorisation department and it will be necessary to obtain land-owners indemnity insurance, as well as the other insurances.

Whatever the size of an event, a club will need to form a committee of keen enthusiasts, all of whom should be perfectionists with a real love for the sport.

The committee should have a chairman who should establish general principles and make the major decisions; ideally he should be experienced in rallying, either as organiser or competitor. However, perhaps the most important post is that of the Clerk of the Course who will be responsible for the route-finding, together with the time schedules and general layout of the event. The Secretary of the Meeting will be responsible for most of the paperwork - production of regulations and so on - as well as for administration during the event and maybe the results team too. An Entry Secretary is a useful addition to the team as he can take one onerous chore away from the Secretary.

A number of co-ordinators, or Sector marshals should be appointed; they will look after certain sections of the route and be able to make emergency decisions in their area on the day of the rally.

In the case of a stage rally a Commander should be appointed for each stage to take control of that section - his counterpart in road rallies will be in charge of a group of controls; great experience is necessary for these people as they can make or mar an event.

A Public Relations Officer is most important as he is the person who makes written and personal contact with many of the people who may well be opposed to the rally. He will need a lot of assistance and ideally should lead a team of articulate, knowledgeable people who will attempt to iron out any route-finding P.R. problems at an early stage, by calling on land-owners and householders before (and in some cases after) the event.

Much of the work takes place *before* the event but on the day or night of the rally it will be absolutely essential to have another important person, the Results Marshal. He should head a team organised to produce speedy, accurate results - these will probably be fed in from various sections of the route by telephone and confirmed by completed documents as the rally progresses.

Other posts which are important though the level may vary according to the size of the event, are Medical Officer, Programme Officer, Chief Timekeeper, and Equipment Officer. All events will also require a Scrutineer and Stewards and these people *must* be fully qualified and fully acquainted with their duties; don't just appoint people under the Old Pals Act. Note that there should be enough scrutineers to avoid queues building up.

Organisers of special stage rallies will need to pay particular attention to medical aspects and in addition to the Chief Medical Officer other medically qualified people should be available and positioned properly. Accidents happen and a stage rally organiser must cover every detail so that any accidents can be dealt with efficiently. Doctors, ambulances, fire appliances and breakdown teams must be available to get to any section quickly and everybody must be aware of the various channels of communication.

Having planned everything in the utmost detail before the event the rally organiser must then be prepared for numerous last-minute changes. Many rally organisers have suddenly found sections of their route impassable because of floods, ice, snow or fallen trees, and competent people must be available to make re-routes and support them with written documentation literally minutes before the arrival of the first car.

Incidentally it makes sense to have someone delegated to promote the event and get publicity for it - if sponsors are involved they may be able to help here. They must liaise with local newspapers and radio stations by supplying them with details of interesting entries etc. They will not only be carrying out a valuable P.R. service for your club and your event, but also for rallying as a whole. They must liaise with any local civic dignitary or Beauty Queen who may be called upon to start the event. In addition they may get involved with the printing of the programmes and a number of very important details which contribute towards the success of an event.

Try not to combine the media promotion with the task of doing P.R. with farmers and householders along the route: they are different jobs. Both are important and need individual attention.

Now let us consider the rally documents. All road books, route cards, time cards and other printed matter must be of high quality, easily read and understood. Be particularly clear and concise in wording instructions and let there be no excuse for misunderstandings. We appreciate that not all rally budgets will run to beautifully printed documents but ordinary duplicating or Xerox prints will be quite satisfactory; just make sure that every sheet handed out is totally readable.

The chapter on rally navigation covered the different types of route instruction; a straightforward list of map references, with directions of approach and/or departure is the most popular form for a road rally. Incidentally, check everything that is printed - a small printer's error could produce absolute chaos with your entire rally entry bogged down in a field!

For special stage rallies the route should be given out in the form of a Tulip road book. Some organisers think that this is not totally necessary and that a few map references will suffice but when competitors are required to visit some stages more than once confusion can easily be caused by the navigator having too many lines on his map. Tulip arrows are simple to prepare and simple to read. Organisers will probably need to make at least two complete trips round the route to collect all the junction diagrams, distances and signpost directions. All junctions and mileages should be put into order and clearly typed, preferably with a clear faced typewriter. The road book must give the competitor all the information for him to complete the route. Like everything else in rallying, the clearer and simpler the better.

In addition to the route, the road book should contain details of relevant telephone numbers, list of controls and special stages, service and rest halts and any other useful information. Procedure at special stages should be reiterated and there should also be special notes about damage, and indeed a damage declaration form, as this will enable any route damage to be traced by the organisers, providing a form has been returned to them.

The marking of special stages is a topic that causes great discussion wherever rally crews meet but again, the most sensible guideline is to make sure that everything is marked clearly and without any ambiguity. The R.A.C. recommend that a Tulip route of each stage should be given to competitors but this may not always be necessary provided *every* junction is clearly arrowed and unused roads are blocked off by logs or taped off.

Advance arrows should be placed approximately 50 yards before a junction (or fire break), but if competitors are likely to be travelling at really high speeds the distance should be increased to give adequate braking distance before the corner.

Arrows on junctions should be placed either side of the road to form a 'gate' through which competitors will pass (be sure to leave them far enough apart so that they do not get knocked over). The arrows should always show the general direction of the exit road using one of the following positions: straight on, 45° right or left, 90° right or left and 135° right or left. It is important that the advance arrows and the arrows on the junctions are identical in the direction in which they point. As mentioned, any road that is not being used should be blocked off and a "no entry" sign placed several metres into the road in case somebody goes along it by mistake. (Be careful with Scottish events — arrows may be at 90°, irrespective of corner angle).

When signposting airfields take particular care to make the route as clear as possible as the number of stories of people lost on airfield stages over the years would fill a book twice this size. One little arrow leaning against a straw bale in the centre of a mile-long runway will not be easily be picked up on a wet and windy night!

Caution boards are important and should be used by responsible rally organisers though not over-used. Some organisers take the view that "all's fair in love and war" and seem to derive satisfaction from seeing expensive cars drop over rocky ledges. Better organisers will place a caution board where there is an obvious chance that accidents will occur and only the most foolish drivers will ignore such boards.

While on the subject of boards let us mention that flying finish and finish-line boards should be positioned intelligently so that cars have enough room to slow down and stop between a flying finish and the stop line.

When a stage has been arrowed and fully set up, at least two cars should travel over the route. One should be driven at a fairly slow speed in order to double check that all is correct and the other should be driven at rally speed to give a competitor's view of things.

Clear reliable time pieces should be used by all marshals and these marshals must be quite clear about their role in the event. They must be familiar with all the time cards which they will have to sign and they must use a consistent method of handling cars. It is no good stage marshals counting some cars down from ten to one, then merely shouting the last three seconds to another car. There must always be an adequate number of marshals at each control.

Marshalling is an important part of rallying and we have already advocated that everyone should have a crack at the job, at least once in their life. Marshals control the progress of an event and, be it a road or stage rally, their efficiency can have a tremendous bearing on the success of a rally. Organisers should give as much information as possible to marshals. Such information should tell them about the event, their responsibilities and details of competitors. It must clearly mark responsibilities - a Stage Finish marshal and a Car Park marshal are totally different beings.

Marshalling can be great fun but just occasionally marshals gain something of a power complex and though marshals are generally the much loved, unsung heroes of rallying there are one or two who do little to endear their club to competitors.

We advocated in an earlier chapter that competitors should be nice to marshals; we suggest that this ought to be reciprocated.

The start of a 'Restricted' rally may lack some of the glamour and razzamataz of an international — but none of the enthusiasm!

Marshals must be absolutely reliable and turn up at briefings and of course control points well in advance of their due times. They should be properly dressed for the occasion and should take plenty of spare clothing as well as umbrellas, spare torches, paper, maps, food and refreshments and anything else that makes the job more comfortable. Marshalling is an interesting job and can be very satisfying as well.

The starting point of a rally is important if things are to go well. The most used rally start areas are garages or large petrol stations, although more important events may start from City Squares, Promenades or even from the Town Hall steps. Whatever starting facilities are chosen make sure that everything is clear and straightforward for competitors and spectators alike. Obviously it is important to have petrol available near to the start and it is usually not difficult to find a garage which will be open specially to offer starting facilities in exchange for the petrol sales. There must be enough room for signing-on and adequate toilet facilities should be available.

How much you dress up the start of your rally depends upon the nature of the event and possibly what sponsorship you have but an informed commentator and P.A. system is always a good thing. Even a few bits of well positioned bunting and a banner or two can add a sense of occasion!

Half-way stops and petrol halts are most important. The rally should be timed to give competitors adequate time for re-fuelling. When selecting a garage for a petrol halt, make sure that they know what they are

Noise complaints can affect the future of road rallying so all cars have to pass a rigid noise check before and during each event. Here a marshal uses an approved decibel meter.

in for and that they have adequate staff as well as adequate change and all necessary facilities. Remember, too, that service cars and spectators will probably wish to fill up, so the petrol pump attendant should not be surprised if his two-pump/wooden shack emporium takes on the appearance of a motorway service station for a while.

Organisers should send someone to petrol halts *well* in advance of the rally - one recent important event collapsed at 3a.m. when the garage owner forgot to open up!

In the case of an all-night rally the hotel or restaurant selected for the finish must have adequate catering and washing facilities and good car-parking space. Motorway service areas are often used although these can be a little impersonal and the rally prizegiving can lose something of its glamour if held in the corridor between the Transport Cafe and the "Gents".

In the case of bigger rallies where competitors and officials will be staying the night it is important to have a good working relationship with hotels selected as starting or finishing points. Many hotel groups now actively encourage rallies to start and finish at their premises.

When the rally has disappeared, all signs of it should have similarly vanished. The sport of rallying will not endear itself to the general public if it leaves a string of empty oil-cans and old racing numbers in its wake.

A good rally can be ruined if results take a long time to appear so it is important that a smooth system is developed to produce results and to keep competitors furnished with information about their performance as the event progresses. Most rallies use telephone links between their headquarters and personnel in the field.

نهاية مرحلة خاصّة – ٤ مراقبين
FINISH OF SPECIAL STAGE – 4 MARSHALS

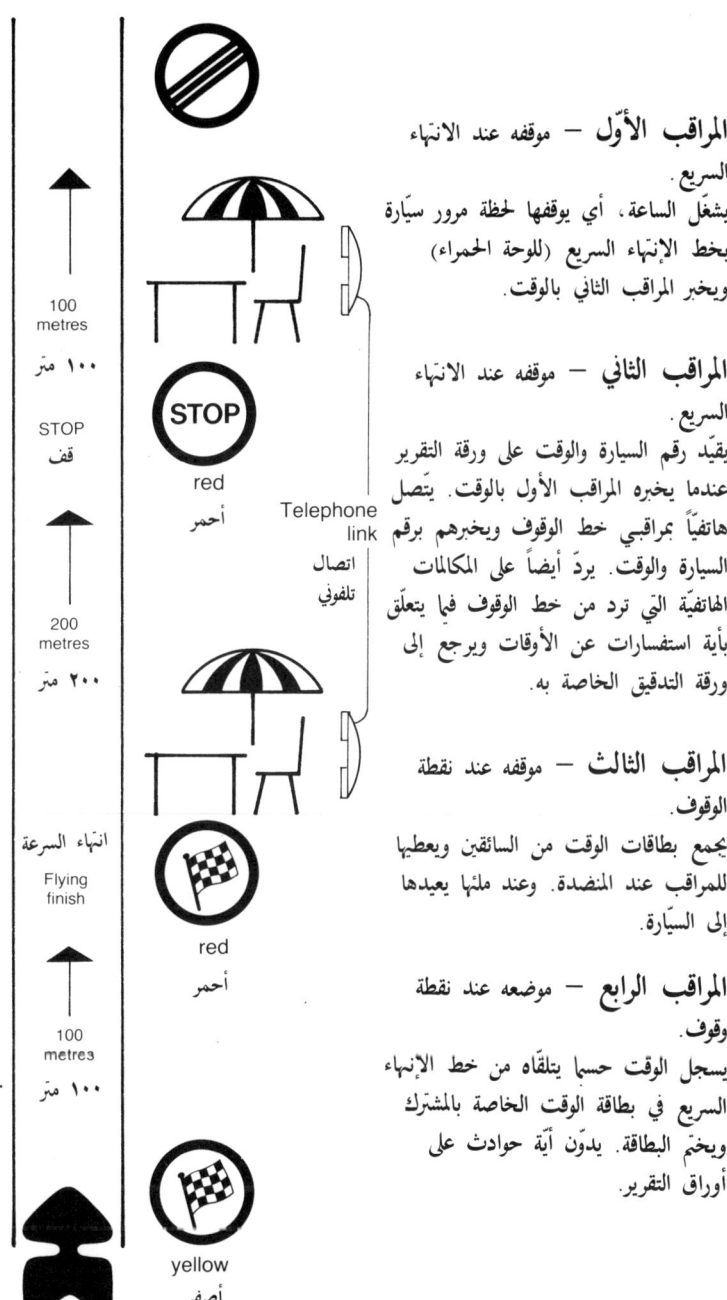

MARSHAL 1 – positioned at flying finish.
Operates clock, i.e. stops it as a car passes the flying finish line (red board) and informs Marshal 2 of the time.

MARSHAL 2 – positioned at flying finish.
Enters car number and the time, as informed by Marshal 1, on the check sheet. Telephone the stop line and informs them of the car number and time. Also answers telephone from stop line regarding any queries of times and consults his check sheet.

MARSHAL 3 – positioned at stop.
Collects timecards from competitor and gives them to Marshal at table. When completed returns them to car.

MARSHAL 4 – positioned at stop.
Enters time, as informed by flying finish line, in competitors time card and stamps the card. Enters any incidents on report sheets.

المراقب الأوّل – موقفه عند الانتهاء السريع.
يشغّل الساعة، أي يوقفها لحظة مرور سيّارة بخط الإنهاء السريع (للوحة الحمراء) ويخبر المراقب الثاني بالوقت.

المراقب الثاني – موقفه عند الانتهاء السريع.
يقيّد رقم السيارة والوقت على ورقة التقرير عندما يخبره المراقب الأول بالوقت. يتّصل هاتفياً بمراقبي خط الوقوف ويخبرهم برقم السيارة والوقت. يردّ أيضاً على المكالمات الهاتفيّة التي ترد من خط الوقوف فيما يتعلّق بأية استفسارات عن الأوقات ويرجع إلى ورقة التدقيق الخاصة به.

المراقب الثالث – موقفه عند نقطة الوقوف.
يجمع بطاقات الوقت من السائقين ويعطيها للمراقب عند المنضدة. وعند ملئها يعيدها إلى السيّارة.

المراقب الرابع – موضعه عند نقطة وقوف.
يسجل الوقت حسبما يتلقّاه من خط الإنهاء السريع في بطاقة الوقت الخاصة بالمشترك ويختم البطاقة. يدوّن أيّة حوادث على أوراق التقرير.

Rallying is new to the Middle East so marshal's instructions tend to be very explicit!

It is sensible to put up lists of penalties at frequent intervals at the rally finish to keep people interested until the full results are posted. Printed sets of results should be mailed to all competitors as soon as possible after the event and it is a courtesy to send them to all the marshals and other interested parties.

Rally organisers are a masochistic breed but, on the whole, a very friendly lot. If you are a beginner and really fancy organising an event - no matter how small - make contact with an established rally organiser in your locality. He will be very happy to put you on the right lines. Rally organisation is an exacting and responsible job as the smallest mistake can have serious repercussions.

As with so many other aspects of rallying, the message is: attention to detail.

11 The classic rallies

There are many good rallies but only a few have that rare mixture of a tough route, some tradition and above all, that intangible ingredient X which gives them magic and makes them classics. These are a few of them:

The Monte

Still has the magic of the name despite occasional organisational lapses over the years which have tarnished the legend among competitors. Very large entries of over 200 cars, mostly privateers.

The rally is split into four sections:

1. *A concentration run from ten or so starting points to Monte Carlo.*
2. *A classification of two or three tests to establish a running order to avoid baulking*
3. *A common run, including twenty classic stages in the French Alps.*

The Monte Carlo Rally. Paddy Hopkirk on the way to a win way back in 1964.

4   The final night. A splendid chase "three times round the mountains" behind Monte Carlo. Usually eleven or so stages, with several runs over the famous Turini. Possibly the finest concentrated piece of motoring in rallying

Save up, enter the rally then dine out on it for months. Not so many Beautiful People about as at the Grand Prix but Monte in January can still be very pleasant.

Although it has its critics the Monte is still one of the best known events in the world. Note the radio aerial for communication with service crews.

From the sublime to the sublime and on to:

The Safari

Some of the mystery has filtered away now that several Europeans have won the Safari but it still remains a tremendous challenge against time and the elements. One of the few rallies not divided into 'stages'. It is one stage from start to finish — usually at an average of over 60mph! Then remember that it is either very, very wet or very, very muddy and you see why it is for men, not boys.

There is always plenty of local interest on the Safari. Note the 'roo bar' to protect the car in close encounters of the unexpected kind with animals.

Dust and dirt roads. A Datsun on Safari.

Now takes place entirely in Kenya and, because of the travel costs, is well nigh prohibitively expensive for European private owners. Mind you, if you can get there somehow you needn't be deterred by the quality of the entry which falls off badly after the first dozen or so cars.

And we nearly forgot: it is worth trying to do the rally just to see the wildlife.

Be prepared for Safari fever – in other words, nerves – which sometimes put even the most experienced drivers on edge. There is no known antidote.

The battles between teams over planes and helicopters are almost as entertaining as the rally – but don't blame them for laying on lavish service when *every* service point is practically a pit stop: if someone passes you while you are at a service point you may have to follow in their dust for miles.

Long may the Safari survive. It probably will – as long as it attracts world interest (including extensive coverage on Japanese TV).

Third on our list for sheer excitement and rated by many as the best rally on the calendar is:

The Lombard R.A.C. Rally

As your 'home' classic this is the one you should work towards in your development as a rally driver. Virtually 'forest racing' with no practising allowed. This causes some concern as many Europeans feel that British drivers have a distinct advantage in getting to know the forests through using them on other rallies – but this doesn't stop Scandinavians winning fairly regularly (which is perhaps why the rally is so popular with them).

One of the world's great rallies – the Lombard-R.A.C. Roger Clark seen here is the only British driver to have beaten the Scandinavians for far too many years.

Recent events have seen a tightening of timing to put it in line with other European events and make mammoth servicing less easy.

Spectator interest has to be seen to be believed. In fact, the enthusiasm causes problems because stages sometimes have to be cancelled because of too many people around!

If you want to get noticed, grit your teeth and try to lead the rally by teatime on the first day. Better still, try to lead it by teatime on the last day.

Timo Makinen, here about to spray the spoils, took a stranglehold on the Lombard-R.A.C. with a hat trick in the 1970s to match Eric Carlsson in the 1960s.

Similar to the R.A.C. in that it takes place over loose roads is:

The 1000 Lakes Rally

This is the Finnish forest Grand Prix and has remained unchanged in character for quite some time. The winners have usually covered colossal practice miles, although pressure from residents on the rally route has lead to strict limits on recce speeds being imposed – could this be a foretaste of what could happen throughout Europe?

'Yumping' on Finland's 1000 Lakes Rally.

If you think of Finns as wild men be prepared for a shock when you see them on the road sections — they are meticulous in obeying speed limits because there are heavy rally penalties for breaking the law; the police have been known to put rally stickers on otherwise plain cars in order to catch people speeding!

You may see marks made on roads on the stages — these are where spectators have wagered who will 'yump' the furthest among their heroes. Regularly 6000 *paying* spectators on stages — very well controlled by marshals with Alsatian dogs.

Never been won by a non-Scandinavian and only three times by a non-Finn. That could be opportunity you hear knocking. The 1000 Lakes no longer really lives up to its reputation — but it would help your career to win it!

The Acropolis Rally.

Our final choice for this somewhat arbitrary list of 'classics' is:

The Acropolis

A great stage event over 2600 km of rough roads and what look like goat tracks. 800 magnificent kilometres of special stages. A qualifying event for six national (as well as the world) championships and usually a big entry.

Very tough, very fast, very demanding but ... don't shy away. Greece is glorious at the time of year and it is an ideal rally to combine with a holiday: take your car down on a trailer because you stand a fair chance of breaking down.

Well, the five rallies listed above will keep you busy for a while but there are others ...

Captain Culcheth at work on the Welsh Rally.

Much less expensive than our famous five is the *24 Hours of Ypres Rally* in Belgium. With two night runs, secret stages and a ban on slick tyres this is an ideal event for someone tackling a foreign rally for the first time.

Even nearer home, the *Welsh* and *Scottish* have a lot of attraction, both being excellent practice for the R.A.C. Rally. The Scottish is rough and you may get through a lot of tyres but it is a super event through glorious country and with a fine social side.

The Welsh is one of the cheapest of the home classics and a 'must' on your way to tackling the R.A.C. Rally.

If Easter in Ireland is your scene then the *Circuit of Ireland* will be high on your list. But don't be lulled by the social side — it is a tough, demanding rally. Tarmac stages on closed roads add to the joy. No practising allowed although obviously the classic stages getwell known, being used year after year.

Some would argue that the *Swedish Rally* is better than the 1000 Lakes. Certainly it is different, being entirely on snow and ice. Funny regulations on studded tyres might mean you need special ones just for the one event which in any case is *very* expensive to do. And it is a lot colder in Sweden in winter, than Finland in August!

Just as the 1000 Lakes and Swedish get compared, so do the Acropolis and the *Rallye du Portugal*. Like the Acropolis this is rough and tough and quite expensive — but then so is any World Championship event if you are going to tackle it properly with a thorough recce.

The *Tulip Rally* used to be a classic for private owners but it has fallen from fame through faulty organisation. Advantages: easy to get to and unpractised stages which reduce costs.

Expensive and a long way away but with a character all of its own is the *Tour de Corse.* Thousands and thousands of corners but curiously if you've done Welsh road rallies you won't feel totally at sea in Corsica. Really a road race in the classic style of a Targa Florio or Mille Miglia.

Expensive (of course) but one of life's more enriching experiences!

Rough and tough — the Scottish Rally.

If you can't stand the cold – stay away from the Swedish Rally.

A Stratos kicks up the dust on the Portuguese Rally.

The Championships

If you find the loot to tackle a programme of big rallies you may get enthralled at the idea of going for a major championship. Our advice? Lie down until the feeling goes away because, sadly perhaps, rally championships don't mean too much.

There are three major championships:

1. World Rally Championship for Makes and Drivers.

Around a dozen qualifying events, including the major five listed earlier. 10 points for first overall, down to 1 point for tenth. Minimum length of the qualifying events must be 2000 km with at least 200km of tests.

A very expensive series to do and few manufacturers tackle this Championship seriously, which makes it difficult for rallying to have the same general public appeal as Formula One, where all cars and drivers do *all* qualifying rounds.

From 1979 the series includes a World Rally *Drivers* Championship — high time, because (hard though it may be for manufacturers to accept it) people *are* interested in people.

2. European Rally Championship for Drivers

Lots of qualifying events – generally shorter than the World Championship ones with a minimum length of 700km of which 150km must be special stages.

Quote: "An award of points, multiplied by the co-efficient of the event, will be made to the best-placed drivers". You can do all the events, although only your best eight scores count, but as soon as you see the word "co-efficient" you know it won't be easy for the public to understand, which perhaps explains the reluctance of manufacturers to tangle with this Championship.

As if those two weren't enough, there is also the:

3. F.I.A. Cup for Rally Drivers

Qualifying events for this are split into three categories:

(A)   Rallies counting for the World Rally Championship.
(B)   The rallies with the highest co-efficient in the European Rally Championship for Drivers, and ...
(C)   Very well known rallies not counting for either of the above e.g., things like the Bandama Rally and the Total Rally in South Africa.

Classifications? Well get this: you count your five best results in Category A rallies, your two best results in Category B and the best result in Category C.

Again, quote: "When the final classification is established, a driver who has participated in no Category B rallies should deduct from his total of points his best result obtained in a Category A rally".

Forget it! Just keep your fingers crossed that the World Rally Drivers Championship *really* means something by the time your talents have come to the boil.

A classic of its kind – the Tour de Corse which can sometimes be …

… sunny and dry – but still very fast and very tough on car and crew.

12 The rally stars

Although rally stars do not receive the public acclaim of the Formula One drivers, they are still idolised by enthusiasts and are often well known sportsmen in their own countries. For instance, Finnish stars have placed in the top three in national sportsmens polls in newspapers.

What follows is a selection of successful rally drivers. The list is not, repeat *not,* exhaustive and because we are devout cowards it makes no attempt to put drivers into any sort of order of merit — it is strictly alphabetical! Having said that however we are certainly starting with one of the quickest:

Markku Alen (Finland)

Markku started rallying in the late sixties and finished third on the 1000 Lakes in 1971 and 1972. He really sprang to attention with an incredible drive on the 1973 R.A.C. Rally — after an accident he dropped to the back of the field after only a few stages. When someone commiserated with him and said "Better luck next year" he sharply pointed out that he hadn't finished with that year's event yet — then fought back to finish third overall!

His results since then, such as his 1000 Lakes wins, have confirmed his talent and that dedication he showed back in 1973.

Pentti Airikkala (Finland)

Another Finn and we are only on our second driver! British rallying received a great boost when Pentti arrived on the scene driving Vauxhalls, Ford then Vauxhalls again on our Championship rallies. He finished a close second in the 1977 British Championship.

He started rallying in 1965 using an old Volvo in Finnish 'junior' rallies then after a brief stab at racing, he rallied with Isuzu, Renault and Opel and at one time was team manager for Opel in Finland.

Always an enjoyable driver to watch, Pentti's main hobby is trials riding along Finnish forest paths, he reckons this keeps him fit for rallying!

Stig Blomqvist (Sweden)

Stig started rallying in the mid-sixties, driving a two stroke Saab and has since become as synonymous with Saab as Eric Carlsson was before him. Really came to notice in 1970 when he led the R.A.C. Rally until a shunt put him out. He made no mistakes the following year, winning nine other major rallies as well as the R.A.C.

The best tribute to Stig is to say that other drivers always want to know what stage times he has done.

Russell Brookes (Great Britain)

If Roger Clark has been the king, then Russell is the Crown Prince of British Rallying. His first event was a University rally in an Austin Westminster – he rolled!

For a few years he navigated on minor rallies – good training – and drove on things like sprints and autocrosses; then from 1968 he started rallying a Mini, scoring class results on the Welsh, Scottish and R.A.C.

Penury looked likely to put him out of rallying when he got a major break — sponsorship to do the Mexico Rally Championship in 1972. He came fourth, then second the following year. Andrews Heat for Hire came on the scene in 1974 and Russell in an RS2000 won the Castrol Autosport Group One Championship.

In 1975 he was loaned a works RS1800 for several important events — including the Scottish on which he finished second. He returned to win it in 1976, along with several other rallies that year. He joined the works team in 1977 and the rest is history — he won the British Championship! He took the Circuit for the second year running in 1978 and his electrifying style has made him very popular with rally enthusiasts everywhere.

Roger Clark (Great Britain)

Let us declare our interest: both authors have known, liked and been involved with Roger for a long time and *both are convinced that he is the greatest British driver there has ever been, or possibly ever will be.*

To list his successes in detail would mean printing a 'part 2' for the book so let's just point out that in the last seventeen years only one man has beaten the Scandinavians on our own R.A.C. Rally. Roger Clark — and he has done it twice (in 1972 and 1976).

One of the most 'complete' men in rallying, it is scarcely a *cliché* to describe him as a legend in his own lifetime. Calm and philosophical and with a wide interest in other activities, including flying and power boat racing.

Andrew Cowan (Great Britain)

Scotland has not just produced great racing drivers — Andrew Cowan is surely the world's greatest long distance rally driver. He won the first 'marathon' in 1968 from London to Sydney (winning the second version nine years later) but in the meantime his name became virtually a permanent fixture at the top of the results of the Southern Cross rally in Australia. He also won the bizarre South American Marathon event in 1978.

An outstanding rally driver and an outstanding ambassador for rallying.

Brian Culcheth (Great Britain)

Another great ambassador for the sport, 'Culch' has been rallying since 1960 and in that time has rallied in over fifty different countries! He has taken high places in many classic rallies — including second overall on the mammoth London to Mexico in 1970. Perhaps the co-driving experience he had earlier in his career helps his methodical approach.

Brian left Leyland at the end of 1977 (after ten years service) to join Opel and his testing ability quickly brought the team major successes, particularly in Group 1 where he won the 1978 Championship.

Ploughs plenty back into the sport with lots of forums and talks to motor clubs — an example for others to follow!

Bernard Darniche (France)

One of Europe's most successful rally drivers — and one who, unlike many French rally drivers, drives with his head. He won the European championship for two years in succession with a privately run team and his name graces the winners list of many major rallies. So it *is* possible to do well as a private owner and walk away with Championships but *only* if you have Bernard's sheer determination.

Timo Makinen (Finland)

The man who took over from Eric Carlsson as the world's best known rally driver. Made his rally debut back in 1959 on the 1000 Lakes in a TR3. Then moved on to a Mini-Cooper and when the Morris importer in Finland persuaded BMC (as it was then) to give him help, his career rocketed.

What can we say about someone who won a Monte Carlo Rally — with a classic drive — in 1965 (to say nothing of the 'lighting year') and then took a hat-trick on the R.A.C. nearly a decade later?

Great sense of humour and although he and Roger Clark have never been close friends, they share a common hobby: power boating.

Hannu Mikkola (Finland)

Rated by many as the fastest driver on the rally scene, Hannu started rallying back in 1963 with a secondhand Volvo. After good drives on the Monte and Acropolis in Datsuns in 1968, he was offered a Ford for the 1000 Lakes — and won. This earned him a contract for 1969 and he again won the 1000 Lakes, as well as the Austrian.

Although Hannu was regarded as a sprint driver he confounded the theorists by winning the 16,000 mile London to Mexico in 1970 but perhaps his most important win (certainly important for European rallying) came in 1972 when he broke the local domination of the Safari.

In the seventies he drove for Toyota and Peugeot, returning to Ford for the 1978 season during which his drives on events like the Welsh and Scottish were awe inspiring.

Sandro Munari (Italy)

Let's let just a *few* of his results speak for themselves: 1972 1st Monte; 1973 European Champion; 1974 3rd on Safari and R.A.C., 1st San Remo; 1975 1st Monte; 2nd Safari; 1976 1st Monte (get's monotonous doesn't it?) 1977 1st Monte, 3rd Safari.

A superstar and particularly formidable at the wheel of a Stratos.

Jean-Pierre Nicolas (France)

Jean-Pierre is perhaps the exception to the rule because in 1978 he won the Monte in a *privately* run Porsche, supported by sponsors. He then went on to win the Safari in the same year, this time in a works Peugeot and then showed that he could shine in yet a third make of car by finishing third in Portugal in an Escort.

Tony Pond (Great Britain)

One of Britain's most talented drivers, Tony first came to prominence via the Escort Mexico Championship. Moving up the power scale he took many worthwhile results in Fords and Opels (including a win on the late Tour of Britain) before switching to Triumph. He scored many successes in 1976 in a Dolomite Sprint in the Group 1 section of the R.A.C. Rally Championship, then towards the end of the year took a TR7 to its first victory on the Raylor Rally. He took the car on to its first International win in Belgium the following year and also finished second on the Scottish.

In case anyone thought he was becoming a 'one-car' driver he made what must be rally history in 1978 when in the space of a few weeks he won the Tour of Ypres in a V8 TR7, finished second on the Mille Pistes in a Group 5 Sunbeam and won a Castrol Rally in South Africa for General Motors! His 1978 Manx win was a fine drive.

Walter Rohrl (Germany)

His country's most outstanding rally driver. After successes in the early-seventies with Ford Capris he switched to Opel in 1973 and scored several wins on Iron Curtain rallies. He became European Champion in 1974 and consolidated his place among the top echelon of drivers over the following years. He won the Acropolis in 1978 in a Fiat.

Gilbert Staepelaere (Belgium)

Gilbert Staepelaere may well have won more international rallies than any other driver in history. With a happy liaison with Ford in Belgium, Gilbert has dominated their domestic championship for over a decade and is some kind of folk hero as a result. He has also featured in a co-driving role with such luminaries as Roger Clark, Timo Makinen and Simo Lampinen.

The rally stars

Ari Vatanen (Finland)

If Ari learns to pace himself properly he will be the major force in rallying over the next ten years. *If,* because at the moment he seems to have only two speeds – flat out or stopped!

An ex-road roller and excavator driver (all budding drivers should have something quotable like that in their background) he started rallying in a well-used Opel and startled the British scene when he brought the car over for the Welsh and Scottish in 1975.

His obvious talent encouraged Ford competitions chief, Peter Ashcroft, to bring him over for the British Championship in 1976. The decision caused considerable comment, which Ari answered in a very simple way – he won the championship!

He tried some tarmac racing while he was in the UK for the year, so it was no surprise when he won the Tour of Britain (which combined circuits and stages).

An enormous talent. If only ... We shall see, we shall see.

We did say at the start that this list was alphabetical didn't we? We hope so because last but by no means least is:

Bjorn Waldegaard (Sweden)

What a driver to complete the list!

Calm, so calm that you don't really expect him to go fast, Bjorn is surely the world's best rally driver with wins (very much in the plural) on rallies like the Swedish, Monte Carlo, Acropolis, R.A.C. and Safari.

He started rallying early – riding in the back of his father's car on rallies at the age of five.

He was driving by the time he was seven but had to wait until 1961 for his first rally when he finished 8th overall – in a national Swedish event – with his father co-driving!

Driving for Scania Vabis, the importers of VW Sweden, he won the 1968 Swedish and became National Rally Champion that year.

As well as rally driving, Bjorn has raced at international level, including a drive on the Targa Florio in a Porsche. Interesting how many of the really top drivers have added racing to their repertoire.

Other names to watch? Plenty of course: any list like this must offend by missing people out, but if you want to study techniques and improve your own results you could do worse than watch drivers like Andy Dawson and John Taylor (both fine instructors incidentally at rally schools) or go and watch Graham Elsmore, Chris Sclater, Jimmy McCrae, Malcolm Wilson, Nigel Rockey or Terry Kaby.

Further afield, John Buffum in America; Vic Preston Jnr, Joginder Singh and others in Kenya; Mike Marshall in New Zealand; Billy Coleman in Ireland – they've all shown they can compete at the highest levels.

Yes, there is a lot of driving talent about but don't let it bother you – there is still room for you if you are quick enough and *if* you plan your progress with care *and* , of course, have some luck.

Billy Coleman   EIRE

Joginder Singh   KENYA

Perhaps the main thing is to keep stretching yourself. *Don't* spend too long at one level of rallying — once you have mastered it, try to move up to another. Go for the events which the team managers will notice — like the one-make championships and if (and only if) you are *convinced* you have what it takes to make it to the top, then concentrate hard on that one aim, if necessary to the point of obsession.

Often at forums we get the comment that rallying is expensive. *Of course it is.* But often the people who make the comment have expensive hi-fi sets, expensive clothes, and expensive girl friends. Hardly the spirit of self-sacrifice and dedication needed to hit the top!

13 Today's great rally cars

Almost all major manufacturers support rallies because of the publicity and development benefits. This is a selection of their rally cars ...

Chrysler

Fiat

Ford

Lancia

Opel

Peugeot

Today's great rally cars

Porsche

Saab

Triumph

Toyota

Vauxhall

But it's not all glamorous – a stop for fuel in Peru during a recce for the Rally of the Incas.

14 Teams, service crews and sponsorship

The team

Like much to do with rallying, *organisation* is the key to a successful rally team. All parts of the team must work efficiently. Nothing must be left to chance. When organising a rally team the most unexpected must always be expected; that may sound "double Dutch" but a professional team will try to plan for every contingency *before* it actually happens. The Team Manager of a professional team will make sure that his service cars carry the most obscure spare parts and everything will have been checked fully and nothing is left to chance.

Even then, some things are totally unforeseeable. Some years ago Timo Makinen and Henry Liddon—one of the most professional crews in the world—made a call for snow tyres for a Scottish Rally. Yes, the sunny Scottish Rally! It was quite unthinkable that it would snow in Scotland in June and Dunlops thought that Ford's Team Manager had taken leave of his senses when snow tyres were ordered. You've guessed—it snowed in the Highlands and covered several stages. Like many Finns, Makinen has a fixation about snow accoutrements and once had snow chains flown out to Kenya to see if they'd work in red murrum mud!

Here we give examples of some of the things that a professional team might organise when competing on a typical international event. On some rallies like the Safari or Monte Carlo there might be special problems needing a great deal of attention; on other events the problems might be simpler. For instance, there might be no tyre choices or no overseas travel to worry about—two of the most time-consuming topics.

If a team is competing on an overseas event all travel movements must be planned in detail. Boat and air tickets should be booked in good time and a travel itinerary be produced.

Plenty of time must be allowed for personnel to get to the start of a rally, particularly mechanics and service cars. Mechanics should be given time to check over cars before the start.

Most teams produce a booklet giving instructions to service crews, ranging from general notes about the positions of service boards and mobile radio to detailed rally car arrival times at service points. Instructions for drivers and navigators will also be included and will cover topics as varied as hotel reservations, emergency telephone numbers and even notes on known sections of route. A team 'Bible' can run to over 150 pages for a complicated international event.

A team should always hold a briefing meeting before the start at which details of each service point are discussed fully so that *everyone* is familiar with his own role on the event. A well-organised team will arrange tickets for post rally functions and may even give advice on dress before and after the event. For instance, team ties, sweaters or blazers help to give a team a tidy, professional image and should be supplied to all personnel if budgets run to it.

Long before an event, an organised team will have numerous meetings where drivers and mechanics compare notes, discuss the rally and its mechanical requirements and make plans in detail. These planning meetings between team managers, drivers, navigators and mechanics always pay dividends.

Service Crews

Throughout this book we have referred to service crews and their importance cannot be underestimated. Although their presence is not strictly necessary and is probably even *unwelcome* on road rallies, there is no doubt that service crews are a necessary part of stage rallying. As speeds of rally cars increase, as stages become rougher and as rallies become longer the more important become the service crews.

There may be a vast difference between the professional works service crew and the amateur, but by describing some of the methods of the former, we hope that amateurs might benefit. To works service crews the rally is a job of work for which they are paid and whilst they are totally dedicated to their job and to the sport, they cannot be expected to do anything 'purely for the love of it'. In other words, they will be reimbursed at the appropriate rate for the job and should be provided with first class equipment.

A good service crew will consist of two or three mechanics in an estate car or van. They will all be skilled and capable of all types of mechanical work, although one or other may have special knowledge of some particular subject, for example: electrics or engines. They will have every conceivable spare part on board although obviously nothing unnecessary will be carried as the weight of the service car is important.

FORD MOTOR CO. LTD.
COMPETITIONS DEPARTMENT

SERVICE SCHEDULE .... R A C INTERNATIONAL ...RALLY

| CREW NO. | 5 | NAMES | J RUSHBROOK/P CHOPPING | DATE | SUN/MON. 23/24 NOV. | COMPETITION NUMBERS | 1, 6, 14 |

SPECIAL INSTRUCTIONS:-

NO.	PLACE	MAP	REF.	ARRIVE BY	FIRST CAR DUE	DISTANCE	TRAVELLING TIME	AVERAGE	COMPETITORS COMING FROM	REMARKS/ROUTE
22	After SS 19 CIRENCESTER PARK In Service Area	163	989 018	12.00	12.35	206m.	–	–		With Crew 1. Approach on A419. Enter Park at Spot Height 126.
29	Before and after SS 25 Yellow crossroads near Round House.	181	985 356	20.15	20.45	88m.	6h 45m.	6mph.	S	Off Route. Go through Severn Bridge Service Area for new tyres from Dunlop.
36	After SS 35 Yellow road 1½m. from ST HARMON	136	016 719	03.58	04.27	145m.	6hrs.	24mph.	E	Off Route.
42	After SS 42 TC 13 BETWS-Y-COED	115	797 559	11.25	11.55	76m.	5h 35m.	13mph.	–	With Dunlop and Crews 2 and 6. Replenish tyres from Dunlop.
47	YORK RACECOURSE Service Area	105	600 497	17.45	18.16	161m.	4h 15m.	37mph. (incl. Motorway)	–	With all other Crews and Dunlop. Full Check. Wash Cars.

A page from a works team Service schedule. Average speeds are kept very low and precise locations of service points are given. A service crew must be able to plot map references and read a map.

The service crew will be prepared to go anywhere providing proper arrangements are made for them and whilst they will have no illusions about their driving abilities they will all be competent drivers in all weather conditions. At least one member of the crew will be equally competent at map reading, and will have the ability to plot references, interpret time schedules and generally keep the service car on the right route.

A good rally mechanic will enjoy the challenge of his work and will cheerfully work in the most outrageous conditions if the success of the team depends upon it. Works mechanics are frequently seen working in sub-zero temperatures or in mud and rain.

To see any real expert doing his job to the best of his ability is a joy, and to see a rally mechanic working with precision at high speed under difficult conditions is as exciting as watching a star driver in full cry; crowds at service points endorse this. Like all professionals, they will take certain precautions and may alter brackets and mounting points to facilitate removal and replacement of parts when valuable seconds count. (Taking care not to break homologation rules, of course). They even make special tools which can get into awkward spots and so save further vital seconds.

Many people think that the life of an international works rally mechanic is one of glamorous jet-setting and mingling with the famous. True, these things do come into the mechanic's life but 90% of his life is pure, solid, honest-to-goodness hard work. He probably enjoys travelling and seeing new places but it is remarkable how quickly mechanics become accustomed to the glamorous surroundings to which their work takes them. Some might think that they are *blasé* to the extreme, but this would be an unfair interpretation. It won't be uncommon to hear two rally mechanics sitting beneath the tailgate of their service car in a remote African village discussing the latest doings of Manchester United or Nottingham Forest.

Service crews must be equipped with the right clothing, whatever climate they are working in. They should always carry at least two pairs of overalls each (one for working in dirty conditions and the other for use at scrutineering and other times when they are not expecting to become covered with mud). They should have good strong boots (some prefer sporting shoes for greater agility), warm underwear and extra sets of waterproof gear. A warm, fur-lined 'Parka' is a good thing to have as well. Don't expect a service mechanic to wear a rally jacket for work and manage to keep it clean—he'll have to be equipped with more than one rally jacket. As we have said elsewhere, oily rally jackets in hotel bars do not present a good team image.

Preparation of the service car or van is almost as important as the preparation of the rally car. First and foremost, it is wise to build a solid grille between the driver's compartment and the rear area, as numerous accidents have happened as a result of jacks, welding bottles or halfshafts flying about inside the car. Furthermore, everything which is heavy should be strapped down. A roof rack is necessary to carry extra wheels and bigger items such as a propshaft or welding bottle. Inside the car there should plenty of small drawers for every conceivable size of nut, bolt and washer. Every drawer and compartment should be labelled and things stored in a logical way.

There should be plenty of light inside the rear of the service car and several spare torches as well as a powerful inspection light which should have a lead long enough to reach right round the car.

Page 1 of 3

TECHNICAL NOTES FOR SERVICE CREWS

Please take special note of the following:

GENERAL	All spares carried in the service cars have to be booked out of Stores on a list.
	At the end of the rally the list will be checked against the items returned.
	Should any of the spares have been fitted to rally cars, the damaged or worn parts which it replaced must be returned to Stores. This is necessary to comply with Auditors' instructions.
FUEL	This year all cars have 15 gallon fuel tanks.
	Service crews must carry five bags in the service cars - and they must be kept full at all times.
	It is unlikely that the rally cars will refuel at many filling stations. They will require frequent refuelling at service points.
WHEELS	Boreham personnel keep an eye on other people changing wheels, and double check where possible. DO NOT OVER-TIGHTEN. Service crews ensure they are carrying an adequate supply of new nuts.
FIRE EXTINGUISHER	A portable manual fire extinguisher is installed in all cars.
ENGINES	Type : 1977 cc.
	Oil : Shell Multigrade
	Ignition Timing : 10°BTDC static 30°-32°BTDC @ 4500 rpm.
	Valve Clearances : .010" inlet .012" exhaust
	Valve Timing : With No: 1 cylinder at T D C on firing stroke, the marks on the inlet and exhaust pulley should line up with marks on the cover. Also the mark on the crank pulley will line up with the mark on the jackshaft pulley.
	Spark Plugs : Motorcraft AG 901 or AG 701. The plug to be used will be painted on the cam cover of the engine. Please ensure all spare plugs are gapped to 0.020" and smear threads with anti-seize compound before fitting.
	Induction System : 48 DCOE Weber carburettors, with foam element air cleaners.

Service crews MUST be properly briefed. Note the comment under wheels about watching over-enthusiastic 'helpers'.

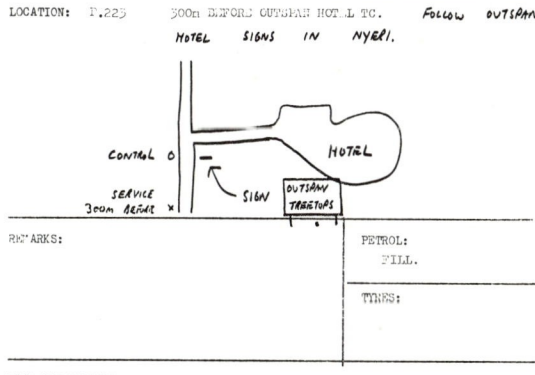

SAFARI RALLY

SERVICE POINT NO:	70	PLACE:	NYERI 'III'
SERVICE CREW NO:	9 & 1.	OTHER CREWS AT SAME POINT: PETROL 4 DUNLOP	
ARRIVE BY:	0600 Mon 11th	FIRST CAR EXPECTED:	0624

ROUTE FOR SERVICE CREW FROM PREVIOUS POINT:

CREW 9 = 340 KM VIA NGI.

CREW 1 = 60 KM

CREW DUNLOP = 90 KM VIA SAGANA.

TOTAL DIST. =   KMS

LOCATION: P.225 300m BEFORE OUTSPAN HOTEL TC. FOLLOW OUTSPAN HOTEL SIGNS IN NYERI.

REMARKS: PETROL: FILL.

                                 TYRES:

TEAM CAR NUMBERS:

Works teams may make a detailed drawing and service sheet for each of the eighty service points on the Safari Rally. These are given to all co-drivers and mechanics in a team.

When a works service crew arrives at its predetermined spot (well ahead of its first potential customer) it will park off the public highway, on level ground if possible. It is common for numerous service cars to cluster together in laybys or service areas, so it is most important for crews to have a good, luminous or even illuminated service board. A simple luminous board is ideal, and should carry the team badge or some simple message or code; long-winded messages are not necessary. A private team's service crew once inadvertently left their service board behind after leaving a service point in a Welsh village. The board was, in fact, a modified racing pit signal kit with removable letters. It was with some chagrin that they discovered their beloved sign, on a return visit to the village, outside a tea shop with the letters re-arranged to advertise cream teas!

Many service crews favour lights on long poles as a method of identifying their location. Hopefully, these can be seen above the rest of the rabble but in reality there are often so many tall poles carrying flashing lights that the view for the approaching rally crews is like that of pilots approaching Heathrow Airport.

When setting up a service point the crew should plan a routine for when rally car arrives. A good rally crew will tell the service crew how much time they have to spare and will then tell them if they have any special requirements. Normally the service crew will be ready to descend on the car for a 'spanner check' underneath the car and a visual check of the engine compartment; this is the normal division of responsibility. The oil and petrol levels should also be checked and all tyres examined for cuts. Spare wheels should be ready, together with jacks and ramps, and if the service crew has advance warning of any necessary repairs they should have every tool and part ready.

A frequent question posed to team managers and mechanics is: "What makes a good rally mechanic?". Basically the mechanic should be technically capable, have a deep interest in rallying and be able to work quickly in difficult conditions. He will like to see his driver succeed in an event and will be unflappable under the most difficult conditions.

Service in style. The Mercedes team took over the workshop of their Adelaide dealers at the half-way stage of the London-Sydney Rally.

Heavy items in a service car MUST be well strapped down to stop them flying into mechanics in an accident.

Sponsorship

Sponsorship came to the rally scene in the late sixties, and although there are differing opinions about the good or bad effect this had on the sport, there is no doubt that it changed it. Furthermore, it helped to establish rallying as a major sport.

There are various levels of sponsorship ranging from free meat from the local butcher in exchange for his name on the side of a club rally car to the sponsorship of teams of cars in huge marathon events where fees in excess of £50,000 might be seen. It is possible to obtain sponsorship for individual cars, teams of cars, single events or even championships.

Most of the major world events are now sponsored by commercial advertisers. They obviously benefit from the publicity brought by hundreds of rally cars, carrying their product name, seen by large numbers of spectators (and perhaps by even more on television or film). All the media, particularly the motoring press, often feature sponsors' names. A wise sponsor will help generate more publicity by arranging special printed matter, advertising material, banners, press releases and even trade or consumer promotions.

On a lesser scale, most restricted and National rallies are sponsored by a wide variety of companies. Organisers who have obtained sponsorship would do well to have an early discussion with their sponsors to establish their aims, their markets and any direct results they are hoping to achieve as a result of the collaboration. For instance in the case of a local stage rally, a sponsor whose marketing area is within the confines of the start and finish points might well feel his expenditure justified just by the local press coverage.

Sponsorship of a local club event could be obtained for £100 or less, or the organisers might offer part-sponsorship in exchange for printing costs. If the sponsorship fee warrants it, the club may offer to incorporate the sponsor's name in the rally title and thereby guarantee the sponsor being mentioned in any media reports. A prime example of this is Britain's major event the much-loved R.A.C. Rally which is now referred to as the "Lombard-R.A.C." thanks to the long-term links between sponsor and organiser. Other major rallies which have changed or altered their names to include sponsor's names are the Mintex Rally in Yorkshire, the Total Rally in South Africa, Spain's Firestone Rally and the Burmah Rally in Scotland. Finland's Hankirally has nothing whatsoever to do with a manufacturer of tissues!

No, not an accident! Just an easy way to work on a car!

Readers of this book will probably be more interested in sponsorship for individual cars and teams rather than events and championships. The only constant factor is the hard work which is necessary to obtain sponsorship then make it effective. A sponsor will not get maximum value from his involvement by merely sticking his name on a car or by tagging it to an event; the sponsor and the sponsored must work hard to obtain every ounce of benefit.

In the case of a private entry sponsored for an event or series of events, it is most important to have the car and crew (and support vehicles, if any) well presented. Providing the fee is sufficient to cover costs, the car should be sprayed and lettered in accordance with the sponsor's liveries and trading styles. A major advertiser working in collaboration with a works team will probably take the initiative but a company that is not so familiar with sponsorship may need some help from the rally crew. A plan should be made and photographs, press releases and other forms of promotional material produced.

Many people abuse sponsorship; it is not simply enough to take a sponsor's fee, plonk his name on your car and rally jacket then leave it at that. Be prepared to appear with the car at fetes or other social functions if the sponsor is likely to benefit—many summer, open-air functions will welcome a rally car as an exhibit. A sponsor should be given due credit at any function (though don't plug him so much that people are put off!) and the sponsor's money should be used wisely. If a sponsor has a particular local area for his business activity, then it is unwise for the crew to concentrate on events at the other end of the country.

The R.A.C. impose restrictions on sponsorship and it is important that people hunting for sponsorship are fully aware of the details. Different licence grades allow different levels of advertising on cars. Basically, a driver/entrants licence allows you to have the name of the entrant, driver and car in lettering no bigger than $4\frac{1}{2}$ inches on the side of the car plus four decals on each side, each up to the size of a shoe box lid.

Any further advertising requires an R.A.C. advertising permit—these cost £25 (Restricted), £50 (National) and £100 for International events. With these licences you can paint almost whatever you like on the car, although nothing obscene of course, old chap. Also, you will have to fork out £20 for an Entrants License if you want your sponsor's name in the rally programme.

The beginner must accept that it is extremely difficult to obtain sponsorship as every advertiser receives countless requests for sponsorship as part of his regular mail. In fact, every commercial organisation receives approaches of some sort every day—many from very worthwhile charities. Even works teams often find it difficult to obtain sponsors and there are hard protracted negotiations before an agreement is reached. A lot of people think that a works team manager merely picks up the phone and call the first large advertiser he can think of—this simply is not so.

Some people produce a leaflet or brochure showing details of their past successes, details of the crew and details of what the combination and proposed programme can offer a prospective sponsor. One thing many people forget is to give an indication of the amount of money involved—they foolishly expect the prospective sponsor to suggest a figure.

Let us end this chapter with a question: what makes you think you *deserve* sponsorship? Rallying doesn't owe you a living and unless you have won something—and something worthwhile—don't expect people to rush to give you money so that you can continue what is after all your sport and hobby.

Finally let us repeat that if you achieve a few wins and as a result get sponsorship then *don't* just take the money and run. Work at the deal and give the sponsor *value.* That way you stand a chance of keeping them for a other year.

15 Crystal gazing...

Hopefully this book will have encouraged you to take up rallying. If it has, you may wonder what sort of future the sport has in store. Well we can't see into our crystal ball for all the sponsor's stickers on it but really we need to look at the future in three steps: short, medium and long term.

In the short term the most immediate task is for the sport to fight harder for itself in the UK to get a proper share of facilities and access to stages. As people have more leisure, sport inevitably will have to be better coordinated – which means committees. Which means that the sport must have proper representation on these committees. If not, we will be frozen out by bikers and hikers, as well as all sorts of other sports. The R.A.C. will have to appoint someone whose sole job is to walk the corridors of power to see that the right representations are made to the right authorities at the right time.

Rallying is *not* a sport we need be ashamed of; it is a sport which gives a lot of pleasure to a lot of people, either as competitors, officials or spectators: we should argue our case for facilities with vigour.

Sadly, at the moment we don't help ourselves very much. Many motor clubs are far too parochial in their approach. There are too many clubs hovering around the 80 or so membership figure and there is far too little liason between clubs. And clubs need to promote themselves and the sport better. How many clubs take an active part in their local community affairs so that they are seen to be responsible people, not just rock apes with noisy, smelly cars? Precious few. How many clubs work with local charities so that they get kindly media coverage in their area? Again precious few.

What has all this hectoring got to do with you, we hear you cry? After all you bought the book as something of a beginner. Well, simply this – those of us who have been in the sport for some time haven't made too good a job of sorting things out. If you come in with a new and fresh approach, you may be able to help safeguard the future of rallying.

Stepping gracefully down from our pulpit, let us consider one or two other short term aspects. Homologation needs sorting out; the hints and innuendoes about cheating just don't help our sport.

Costs need to be kept down. If someone of eighteen wants to be a footballer he need spend little or nothing on equipment; if he wants to be an athlete he could nearly run in his bare feet. If he wants to be the next Roger Clark, somehow or other he has to get behind the wheel of a car. The more we can do to make it easy for him the better ... Let's see more 'one make' formulae, with the rules tightly written to keep expenses to a minimum. It goes without saying that anyone caught cheating should be slung out for a year.

Touch wood, but the spectator control problem seems no worse than it was a year or two ago. However, the speeds of the cars keep going up so we would like to see the introduction of some form of power-to-experience formula. It could perhaps be done via a restrictor plate but *somehow* we must make it impossible for an absolute beginner to enter a rally in a full-house works replica. No one would expect to leap into Formula One without experience. Why should they do so in rallying? One, or two simple power-to-experience formulae would give rallying the equivalent of the Formula Ford, F3, F2 stepping stones into F1. Ford's Peter Ashcroft was thinking along these lines when he introduced his relatively low-cost 1300 Escort Championship.

We remain reasonably optimistic about road rallying. If it ruthlessly disciplines itself it can have a future, although sadly it will never more be studied for stars by team managers.

In the medium term, much depends on the Common Market. Yes really, because inevitably any legislation passed on the motor vehicle is going to affect rallying.

Private tuners are going to find it increasingly difficult to get through legislation, which will leave manufacturers with a stranglehold on what is or isn't allowed. And we will almost certainly be pushed more and more towards standard cars for rallies, maybe even more standard than today's Group 1.

Spectators should not despair though because the works cars will still be a fine sight in full cry. The move towards standard cars will narrow (though not completely close) the gap between private and works teams.

Before the shift to standard cars finally takes place we may see the cost of current Group 4 cars forcing much smaller entry lists, with almost a rally circus rather like Formula 1, with starting money and all the trappings. It won't be a particularly good thing and it won't last long.

Long term? Your crystal ball is as good as ours. It all depends on energy resources. Much as we all love rallying and much as we all shout about its benefits, we have to face facts. And the facts are that if people are shivering under blankets because they have no oil for central heating, then there is no way we will be rallying. We'd be lynched if we tried.

But it won't come to that. Man's love affair with mobility via the motor car is a deep and long lasting one. Man's ingenuity and drive will therefore lead him to overcome any energy problems we may see looming at the moment. And if we still have transport, a select band will still want to go faster to test themselves (there is no sign that the human race is losing its healthy desire for excitement).

And if man still wants to go fast, then there will still be races and rallies. Come to think of it the way some roads are being maintained at the moment, rallying will be more challenging because the roads will be rougher!

We make no attempt to forecast *what* means man will use to continue motoring. It is difficult to see Tony Lanfranchi in 2001 (*of course* he will still be racing) going round Paddock Bend with a sail sticking up out of his car and if we ever have electric cars then we will need a whole new breed of noise marshals—people to check that cars register at least a certain *minimum* noise level—if they don't they will be so quiet that spectators won't hear them coming, which will be dangerous!

To study the future, it is helpful to study the past. If you look back twenty years or so, rallying wasn't all that different then. You could find your way around quieter areas of the country today with the maps in use then and techniques with pace notes, servicing and so on have not advanced much since the early-sixties; some of the stars of the sixties are still rallying, and rallying successfully (which is why there are such golden opportunities for a young person like you—they *must* retire sometime).

We remain optimistic. Rallying will stay healthy at least until the turn of the century. Have fun!